PRACTICING FORGIVENESS

PRACTICING FORGIVENESS

A Path Toward Healing

Richard S. Balkin

OXFORD
UNIVERSITY PRESS

OXFORD
UNIVERSITY PRESS

Oxford University Press is a department of the University of Oxford. It furthers
the University's objective of excellence in research, scholarship, and education
by publishing worldwide. Oxford is a registered trade mark of Oxford University
Press in the UK and certain other countries.

Published in the United States of America by Oxford University Press
198 Madison Avenue, New York, NY 10016, United States of America.

© Oxford University Press 2021

Library of Congress Cataloging-in-Publication Data
Names: Balkin, Richard S., author.
Title: Practicing forgiveness : a path toward healing / Richard S. Balkin,
The University of Mississippi .
Description: New York : Oxford University Press, 2021. |
Includes bibliographical references and index.
Identifiers: LCCN 2020010469 (print) | LCCN 2020010470 (ebook) |
ISBN 9780190937201 (hardback) | ISBN 9780190937225 (epub)
Subjects: LCSH: Forgiveness. | Interpersonal relations.
Classification: LCC BF637.F67 B35 2020 (print) | LCC BF637.F67 (ebook) |
DDC 155.9/2—dc23
LC record available at https://lccn.loc.gov/2020010469
LC ebook record available at https://lccn.loc.gov/2020010470

1 3 5 7 9 8 6 4 2

Printed by LSC Communications, United States of America

To my mother,

Susanne Balkin

"It was very easy to get on her shit-list; it was
even easier to get off it." —Robert Balkin

and

To those who shared their journey with me.

CONTENTS

CONTENTS

PREFACE

The topic of forgiveness is one that resonates. We will all experience relationships that enrich our lives or are a source of distress, pain, or even trauma. When our relationships are strong and healthy, our lives are more vibrant, and when our relationships fall short of our expectations or even are harmful, our lives are filled with challenges and personal struggles. In any event, few relationships in our lives are perfect. Inevitably, we may be let down by the people we count on most, and how these relationships are eventually reconciled or abandoned is the subject of this book.

Every book is written for a particular audience. I struggled to define for whom I was writing this book. On one hand, I believe the forgiveness journey is a universal one, and there was nothing in this book that was a professional secret and could not be shared with anyone wishing to gain insight or evaluate their feelings about forgiveness. On the other hand, after talking to counseling professionals from across the country, I believed I had put together a helpful model and instrument that could be beneficial to their practice and work with clients struggling with issues of conflict and forgiveness. Ultimately, I hope this book bridges both audiences.

Although forgiveness is a universal construct, the manner in which we address conflict and forgiveness is distinct, and perhaps each situation has unique elements that make generalizing any model or behavior difficult or complicated. How you feel about one person who breaks a promise or fails in a relationship may be totally different from how you feel about another person who behaves in a similar manner. Context matters, and the reader is encouraged to look at each situation from a perspective of the special circumstances that might affect the relationship and to refrain from labeling oneself as a forgiving or unforgiving person.

Nevertheless, in this book, I present a perspective on interpersonal and intrapersonal forgiveness. Most readers are probably familiar with interpersonal forgiveness, in which traditionally two people work to overcome breaches or conflicts in their relationship stemming from an offense, harm, or pain that one inflicted on another. In this case, a transgression is forgiven, and a relationship is reconciled. Intrapersonal forgiveness may be a new element to consider for many readers. Intrapersonal forgiveness is an individual journey, in which forgiveness is sought, not through reconciliation, but rather through a desire to relinquish feelings of ill will toward the offender, but not necessarily involving the offender in the process. In other words, intrapersonal forgiveness is within oneself. Sometimes, reconciliation and the renegotiation of a relationship is not healthy or not possible. Intrapersonal forgiveness is addressed as way of moving forward to promote self-healing.

Stories are used throughout the book to describe various processes and conflicts that individuals may face in their forgiveness journey. Some of the stories highlight trauma and difficult, painful journeys. It is not necessary that all issues related to conflict and forgiveness include pain and trauma. Sometimes, we address forgiveness for minor problems or inconveniences, such as, "I am sorry I forgot to pay you back," or "I was not entirely honest about why I was late." Smaller issues may affect a relationship, and the reader is encouraged to keep this in mind throughout the book. A brief description of each chapter follows.

Chapter 1, "Harmful Messages and Pressures to Forgive," introduces the forgiveness journey. Forgiveness is a process, and some of the issues involved in working through the forgiveness journey are highlighted. Descriptions of interpersonal and intrapersonal forgiveness are featured.

Some of our ideas about forgiveness come from long-held beliefs and practices stemming from our background, such as our ethnicity and race, religion, and personal and family values. These and other various facets of culture are explored in Chapter 2, "Forgiveness and Culture: Beliefs and Conflicts." We examine the impact that culture can have on our beliefs about forgiveness and conflict and the decision to move forward in interpersonal or intrapersonal forgiveness.

The Forgiveness Reconciliation Model (FRM) is a primary component of this book and is introduced in Chapter 3, "The Forgiveness Reconciliation Model: An Overview." The FRM was initially developed from a Jewish conceptualization of forgiveness but is considered a transcultural model, having broad applications across various cultures and secular beliefs and practices. The FRM is compared and contrasted with other forgiveness models.

The FRM is a four-phase model that is broken down in subsequent chapters:

- Chapter 4, "Collaborative Exploration"
- Chapter 5, "The Role of Reconciliation"
- Chapter 6, "Remorse and Change"
- Chapter 7, "Choosing the Outcome"

An essential component to the FRM and an added feature of this book is the Forgiveness Reconciliation Inventory (FRI). The FRI was initially designed as a clinical tool to aid in addressing issues of conflict and forgiveness between a client and counselor. However, the FRI can be self-administered. An explanation of administering, scoring, and interpreting the FRI is included in Chapter 8, "The Forgiveness Reconciliation Inventory." A copy of the measure and scoring profile is included in Appendix A.

Finally, Chapter 9, "Does This Work?" provides the evidence for this model from existing research. An attempt is made to address the research findings in a meaningful way without relying on professional jargon and overly technical information. This chapter hopefully conveys information about why this method of addressing forgiveness may be effective for you or the clients you serve. For those who wish to understand the psychometric properties of the FRI, a summary of the technical information is in Appendix B, along with references from professional literature.

I hope that that this process of addressing conflict and forgiveness and the tools provided have a positive effect on those taking this journey. Addressing every conceivable nuance in this process is impossible, but hopefully you have found information that is helpful to you. My very best wishes on your journey.

—Richard S. Balkin, PhD, LPC, NCC

ACKNOWLEDGMENTS

Writing this book required extensive feedback from individuals who provided guidance, enthusiasm, and insight. I owe a huge debt of gratitude to Dr. Michelle Perepiczka, who read every chapter and provided insights, suggestions, and validation for what I was trying to convey. Thank you is not enough. You are gold.

John Afamasaga has been an enormous supporter of and contributor to this book—believing in the value of the project and filming a documentary about it. Thank you for your assistance in developing and promoting this work. Our conversations facilitated the writing, invoked ideas, and promoted my creativity and belief in this project. Thank you, my friend.

I also want to thank Dr. Nephaterria Harris and Reverend Clarence Harris for their guidance addressing the religious and cultural aspects of forgiveness.

At least half of this book was written at Cups in Oxford, MS. Thank you for the ambience, support, and friendship. A special thanks to Matt Mahaffey for helping make this happen.

No set of acknowledgments is complete without thanking my wife, Melissa, and my children, Abigail, Gabriela, and Isabel. Melissa, you are such a big part of this journey. I love you.

Finally, I want to thank my publications editor, Dana Bliss, for his belief in and optimism about this project.

Harmful Messages and Pressures to Forgive

Perhaps more than any other problem or concern that human beings encounter, it is our relationships that contribute to our happiness or are the root of our distress. And our relationships are not simple! They are quite nuanced and complex. Within moments, in a single relationship, we can move through a spectrum of emotions—from happiness to anger to sadness. When a relationship changes because of hurt, injustice, trauma, or trust, the presence and permanence of that relationship may change or even end. At some point, we all experience being hurt by someone, and maybe you can look at a single moment in that relationship when you decided, *I forgive you.*

But sometimes forgiveness is a journey. Time may need to play a role. In those moments when someone has been hurtful and you are in pain, you just need time to confront it, deal with it, and figure out how to move forward. When a relationship has been ruptured, maybe because of deceit or some type of inflicted pain, the nature of the transgression has not changed, but your beliefs about the transgression may change over time. I think about the times when I have worked with clients who have suffered a terrible trauma. Very often, the client cannot summon the words to describe what happened. The mere thought of addressing the event creates tense-ness and inner turmoil. Sometimes, we will just sit with that pain together. The client may cry or yell until such a moment arises that the client can collect the words to describe what has happened. And in that moment, what seemed like an unspeakable trauma has been decreased to something that can be confronted, processed, and healed. In that moment, the client has moved forward in a journey toward healing.

But does this healing imply forgiveness? That's a much tougher question, and as with any complex question, it just depends. It depends on how we define forgiveness. Sometimes, forgive-ness is viewed as an event. In various religions, cultures, and daily interactions, the act of forgiveness takes place at a single moment. In Judaism, for example, there is Yom Kippur, the Day of Atonement, when an individual spends a full day fasting, praying, and reflecting in an effort to be forgiven for transgressions against G-d.[1] Yom Kippur ends with a break-fast, which celebrates an opportunity to begin anew and attempt to better ourselves and those in our lives. But such events do not have to be so regimented. A child who gets upset and defiantly yells at a parent may be told to apologize. Maybe you have seen this occur, or this occurred with your child, or you were the child! The child then tearfully approaches the parent, gives the parent a hug, and says, "I'm sorry." The depth of under-standing may not be understood by the child, but the gesture is appreciated nonetheless. In this moment, we see a parent teaching a child how one takes responsibility for behavior and attempts to make things right.

The reality is that forgiveness is not a simple issue; it is rather complex. Such was the case in my work with Sheila, a 16-year-old teenage girl who was admitted to an acute care psychiatric hospital because of trauma, depression, and feelings of suicidality. Sheila was a victim of sexual abuse by her father. She had endured years of abuse before she finally came forward and informed a teacher about her father's abuse. The teacher informed the school counselor, and a report was filed with Child Protective Services (CPS). From that point, a series of actions and events took place that resulted in Sheila being admitted to an adolescent psychiatric unit.

As with cases related to abuse and neglect involving minors, the perpetrator often denies the allegations, and this was the case with Sheila's father. When I work with adolescents like Sheila, I will let them know that often it feels like things get worse before they get better, but things will get better. After a report was made to CPS, a police officer began an investigation and interviewed Sheila within 24 hours of the report. Soon after, the father was removed from the home. Sheila's mother was caught off guard by the entire scene and felt conflicted in choosing to believe her daughter's allegation or her husband's denial. Sheila became very distressed, felt the ensuing chaos was her fault, and began expressing a plan to harm herself. The CPS case worker recommended that Sheila be evaluated at a hospital, and Sheila was subsequently admitted to a crisis care unit.

I was eventually requested to testify in court related to this case. During the hearing, a prosecuting attorney asked me questions related to my degree, experience, and work with Sheila. The prosecuting attorney made me sound like an expert—that my degree, experience, and perceptions of my work with Sheila mattered. Then, the defense attorney took over. In representing the father and alleged perpetrator, the defense attorney asked me, "Why do you believe Sheila is telling the truth?" I told the defense attorney the following:

> I look for three things. First, I look for *consistency*. By the time
> I have reached a stage like this where an adolescent is admitted in

to a psychiatric hospital and assigned to me, I have documentation about what has occurred from a variety of sources. I have what the client reported to the police officer. I have the CPS report. I have what was disclosed on the preadmission assessment. I also have documentation from the nursing assessment and the admitting physician's history and physical. By the time I sit down and do my initial session with the client and ask, "What is your understanding about why you are here?" the client has told her story and relived her trauma five other times. Sheila's story has remained consistent.

Second, I look for *feasibility*. Does what I am hearing from the client sound feasible? Does it sound like other stories that I have heard? Unfortunately, it does. Working on an adolescent unit, I have heard this story too many times. This happens, and the way it has happened in Sheila's case is consistent with how it has happened for other teenage girls.

Finally, I look for *congruence*. By congruence I mean I expect the client's affect or display of emotion to correspond to what she is telling me. A congruent response might be one of two displays of emotion. Some victims of abuse display emotional detachment. They explain what happened in a very detached way, as if they are in shock explaining the traumatic event. Other victims, and this was the case with Sheila, display sadness, depression, anger, or tearfulness when disclosing the trauma that was endured. An emotionally incongruent response might be someone recalling such trauma with a smirk or with laughter. That does not immediately mean the client is being untruthful. It could be a coping mechanism, but it is much less common and may indicate other issues at work.

So, that is what I look for, and in this case, I have noted all three indicators of why I believe the client. Her disclosure has remained consistent; her story is feasible; and her affect has been congruent with the trauma she has disclosed.

You may have heard the old saying that an attorney should never ask a question for which the answer is unknown. This is probably one of those cases in which the attorney did not heed that wisdom because he seemed genuinely caught off guard. Ultimately, the allegations were founded, and the father was placed in prison.

But this is a book about forgiveness. And I can imagine you reading this story and thinking to yourself, please do not tell me that all was forgiven! Sheila's story conformed to my adage that this situation was going to get worse before it could get better.

A standard protocol of care for adolescents admitted to a psychiatric hospital is to have family sessions. For Sheila, this included sessions with her mom. Sheila had been in the hospital for about 2 days when I met with her and her mom together. I met Sheila's mother in the family conference room, introduced myself, and talked with her about Sheila's disposition so far—feeling depressed and focused on the trauma she has endured as well as feeling guilty about her father's removal from the home. I noted the importance of being supportive and that Sheila was worried about this visit. Sheila's mother was anxious to see her daughter, so I promptly brought Sheila in to the session. They embraced for a few moments. There might have been some tears shed. Sheila sat on a sofa to my right. Sheila's mom selected a chair to my left, and it was interesting to me that she chose to sit across, and not next to, her daughter on the sofa.

Sheila's mom started the session. She looked at her daughter, sat upright, and said, "You know as a Christian you have to forgive him."

Sheila looked down at her feet. I turned to Sheila's mom and said, "Wouldn't that be convenient for you?"

Sheila's mom gave me a glaring look, which I interpreted as, "How dare you!" Actually, I interpreted something a little different, but I am not sure such language would be suitable for a book of this nature.

I calmly followed up my comment. "Well, then you would not have to choose between your daughter's disclosure and your husband's denial, because if everything is forgiven, this could all just go away."

Yeah, Sheila's mom was pretty angry at this point. Again, "angry" probably does not convey the magnitude of the emotion she had toward me in that moment. Can I say "pissed"? Let's go with that. Sheila's mom was pissed. The interactions between Sheila and her mom were minimal after that, and the session ended soon thereafter, with Sheila requesting to go back to the unit. Sheila was tearful but also expressed appreciation that I spoke up for her. I felt compelled to advocate for Sheila. However, not all clinicians agree with the manner in which I confronted Sheila's mom. Any potential working alliance I was to develop with Sheila's mother was certainly ruptured and not likely to be repaired under the structure of a brief, psychiatric hospitalization.

Once, when I was presenting on this topic and told this story, I had a clinician in the audience say to me, "I don't like what you said to the mom." I explained that I understood, but I also felt compelled to advocate for Sheila. The clinician continued to challenge me, "I still do not think that was the right thing to say." So, I responded: "I understand that you do not like what I said. And I understand the ramifications of saying to the mom, 'Wouldn't that be convenient for you.' And while I stand by it, I will not likely convince you that I said the right thing. I am sure there are better things to say. But that's what I said. That's the story. And I am not changing the narrative simply because you do not like it."

So, right or wrong, that comment, "Wouldn't that be convenient for you," set the stage for what was to follow—Sheila going to court, the father going to jail, and the eventual placement of Sheila outside the home. But there was still something that bothered me. It was the statement coming from Sheila's mom in the beginning of the session, *"You know as a Christian you have to forgive him."*

THINGS WE DON'T FORGIVE

There are two parts of the previous statement that are worthy of attention. The first part *"You know as a Christian. . . ."* Honestly, that statement was interesting to me because I am not Christian. I am Jewish! But the idea that the expectations of forgiveness are embedded in religious, spiritual, and cultural ideologies is an important consideration, which we will explore in Chapter 2. The second part of this statement, *". . . you have to forgive him,"* identifies forgiveness as some sort of mandate, and this, I believe, is problematic.

Consider that what a person forgives is quite a unique process. Let's say you have a friend with whom you go out to lunch, and you take turns buying each other's lunch. At some point, you realize that you are paying for more lunches than you are receiving. You may not end the relationship over this, but what if it happens repeatedly? At some point, you might decide, "I have had enough," despite the fact that nothing life-changing has occurred. Yes, it is mildly perturbing, but it is not life-threatening. People have forgiven others for far worse. You have likely forgiven others for far worse. But you just cannot get past this. You feel used, and you decide you are no longer having lunch with this person.

Here is another story: After my Bar Mitzvah (a Jewish coming-of-age ceremony for 13-year-old boys), we had a reception at the synagogue, and my mother served smoked turkey. During the reception, Arthur Mendelsohn approached my mom and said, "Susie, this is great ham!"

My mother was flabbergasted. The idea of serving pork, a non-Kosher food, in the synagogue was deplorable, and her response to Arthur expressed this. "Ham? In the synagogue? Are you crazy? You think I would do that? It's smoked turkey!"

Thirty years later, at my daughter's Bat Mitzvah, she would still tell the story: "Arthur Mendelsohn actually thought I was serving ham at Ricky's Bar Mitzvah. I would never serve ham in the synagogue!" I am not sure my mother ever forgave poor Arthur, and if she did, she certainly never forgot.

And then there is a more nefarious reason to not forgive: Sometimes being angry is powerful. We see this a lot with couples. For example, one person may withhold sex and intimacy because this a way to exert control over the relationship or even enact revenge over major problems like infidelity or over less severe transgressions like spending time on the phone or computer rather than engaging. In some cases, offering forgiveness might mean losing power, and that can be uncomfortable and even a source of vulnerability.

Refusing to forgive might even be fun. Maybe at one time or another you held a job in a very unhealthy work environment, where there was a coworker, colleague, or supervisor (or maybe all of the above!) whose behavior led to your leaving that job. Did you make amends with everyone before you left? Or, did you wish for some karma over the situation, maybe thinking, "They deserve what they get." And doesn't that feel good, to some extent? Perhaps you have even forgiven people who have committed much more severe transgressions upon you, yet you still hold onto this one. Why? Could it be that you actually enjoy it? Or maybe for whatever reason, you feel empowered by leaving, and you want to hold onto that feeling. We often see a similar situation in divorce. Some divorced couples will never forgive each other. Sometimes, holding onto that feeling of empowerment when ending a relationship may feel like strengthening resolve. Forgiveness is not a mandate, and there can be reasons, both compelling and trivial, to not forgive. The real question is whether holding onto this resentment is helping you or hindering you.

Who we forgive and what we forgive vary from person to person and situation to situation. An acquaintance who comes to your house and takes something might never be welcome in your home again, but if a family member committed such an act, say a sibling, cousin, nephew, or niece, what would you do? Would you ban the family member if it were a single occurrence? Would you forgive the person if that person confessed and apologized? The answer to this is, probably, *it depends*. Rather than attempting to define yourself as a forgiving person or unforgiving person, consider the circumstances and the people involved. Forgiveness is situation-specific. Thus, we do not define ourselves as forgiving. Rather, we look at each unique situation and identify what might be in the best of interest of ourselves and the people around us. And sometimes, particularly with the case of Sheila, what is in her best interest is not necessarily what is in the best interest of her mother. Issues of forgiveness are not only complex but also sources of both interpersonal and intrapersonal conflict.

The *interpersonal conflict* (i.e., conflict with others) is a result of the conflicting feelings between Sheila and her mother. Sheila's mother would like for all of this to be swept under the rug. If Sheila would simply forgive her father, the family could be reunited; the pressures of paying bills would be alleviated; and the picture of what a family looks like, according to Sheila's mother's perceptions, would be maintained. However, this is not in Sheila's best interest. Sheila was in an unsafe position. It took a lot of courage for her to come forward. Moreover, the secret is out. There has been an investigation and a court hearing. Sheila's father abused his child, and he will go to jail. Sheila needed to protect herself from further harm, and her mother is not providing the support she requires.

Sheila faces a lot of *intrapersonal conflict* (i.e., conflict within oneself) as well. The rupture of her family weighs heavily on her. She feels guilty that "everything is falling apart." Even though Sheila did the right thing coming forward, she is not getting the support she needs from the people who are most important in her life. Naturally, she questions her decision to come forward about the abuse.

It makes sense that Sheila is resistant to her mother's insistence that she forgive her father. But the process is confusing and potentially fraught with conflict. *"You know as a Christian you have to forgive him."* Consider the innumerable reactions to this statement. There is a religious and cultural context to this statement. We hear colloquialisms embedded in religion and culture quite often, such as "to forgive is divine" or "turn the other cheek." Perhaps you were taught benefits of forgiveness, such as a freedom from emotional burden, decreased stress, spiritual connection, or reconciled relationships. These are powerful beliefs, and when beliefs about forgiveness are deeply held, moving forward may feel less like a choice and more like a sense of obligation. Consider individuals who choose to remain in an unhealthy marriage, even when a spouse is abusive or cheats. Perhaps this choice is not about decreased self-esteem of someone being victimized but rather about a moral imperative. The decision to maintain the marriage could be about a sense of duty or that the marriage is a sacred covenant. Hence, forgiveness is complex and multifaceted.

INTERPERSONAL FORGIVENESS

So far, in these examples, we have focused on interpersonal forgiveness. *Interpersonal forgiveness* is a process in which the "the victim abandons negativity toward the perpetrator and attempts to reconcile the relationship."[2,3,4] Interpersonal forgiveness is a relational endeavor in which a relationship may be reconciled—a perpetrator may offer an apology, and a victim may offer forgiveness.[5,6,7,8] Forgiving a philandering spouse or reconciling with a family member who has struggled with alcohol abuse can be regarded as interpersonal forgiveness. Because interpersonal forgiveness is a relational process, the willingness of two people to work together is essential, and the fundamental components within this relational process include trust and mutuality.

Trust

We all know what trust is, and you can probably think of examples in your life when trust has been maintained or broken. The decision to re-engage with someone who has caused you harm hopefully means that you trust that the person who has caused you harm is not going to do so again. In the best-case scenario, redeveloping trust in a relationship will lead to a long, fulfilling, and interpersonal connection. But this is not always the case! Many times, people choose to re-engage in a relationship for reasons besides trust.

Forgiveness may be convenient. Consider the case of Sheila again. Her mother is asking her to forgive her father. Clearly, if Sheila does not trust her father, sincere forgiveness is not possible. Sure, she could say, "I forgive him," but these words might be spoken in an attempt to bring peace to the family or as a matter of convenience to her mother or father. And could you really blame her? Sheila is facing court battles; her father is being prosecuted and will go to jail; and her mother does not have a job, so how will they make ends meet? Sheila's mother verbalizes disbelief in what has occurred. All of this could go away if Sheila would retract her allegation and change her story. Of course, Sheila's safety should never be compromised. Sheila should have the opportunity to grow and develop in an environment that is caring, compassionate, and safe. But with the pressures noted previously, empathizing with Sheila and other victims of abuse is important because the pressure to retract and compromise safety is real.

When we move outside of our case example and apply the relational concept of forgiveness to our own lives, maybe we can understand that we feel pressure to forgive in order to preserve relationships based on *how we want them to be* versus *what they truly are*. The decision to re-engage in a relationship may be an attempt to pursue an interpersonal connection that will be fulfilling to everyone involved, and in the present moment a victim may not be ready or willing to abandon this relationship—to essentially say, "This relationship will never be what I want or need it to be."

Forgiveness may prolong or avoid an undesirable outcome. Sometimes, we refer to this as *poor reality testing*: We expect a different outcome despite doing the same thing over and over, or we fail to see the logical and natural consequences. When you re-engage in a relationship, you are taking a risk, which can be rewarding or detrimental. Sometimes, you might know that a relationship is not going to work, but the desire to continue to engage in a detrimental relationship might seem more positive than having no relationship at all. The long-term outcome is the same (i.e., ending the relationship), but maybe you think you have some control over when the relationship ends.

Keep in mind that consequences can vary. For example, being in an unhealthy relationship can be emotional and stressful because of constant fighting or emotional neglect. But, being in an abusive relationship can be dangerous. In the former case of being in a relationship that is toxic, you could withstand the stress, but in the latter case of an abusive relationship, you may need to get out because of safety concerns.

More important, consider the balancing act of avoiding short-term discomfort by maintaining the status quo versus choosing the discomfort of making a change or transition. Changes and transitions may be difficult but still the healthier option. The long-term consequences of maintaining an unhealthy relationship can have serious ramifications. People often want progress but do not want to change.[9] Maintaining the status quo (i.e., choosing to maintain an unhealthy relationship) in order to forgo short-term discomfort could have a detrimental or depressing impact on your life.

Forgiveness may seem like an escape from past trauma. Victims, particularly child and adolescent victims, may succumb to the pressure of others, especially family, for the purposes of being obedient, compliant, or attempting to somehow erase the past and the traumatic events that have occurred. Sheila could think, "If I forgive him, then I could just forget that all of this bad stuff ever happened." Such a move might "keep the peace" and lend temporary relief to a disturbing, chaotic, and unhealthy situation. But once again, an attempt to forgive for reasons outside of trust presents a strong likelihood of continued abuse and trauma.

As you can see, there are all sorts of reasons that people choose to re-engage in relationships when trust is not present. And even when trust is present, that does not necessarily translate to a fulfilling relationship or deep, interpersonal connection. You can trust that someone is not going to hurt you, but that does not mean you have abandoned all negative feeling toward that individual. There are additional interpersonal processes that should be considered.

Mutuality

In a mutual relationship, each person is aware of the other's thoughts and feelings and considers them of value. *Mutuality* refers to an equal, empowering relationship that emanates from a "special awareness of the other's subjective experience." [10] When interpersonal forgiveness is pursued and a relational process ensues, two people can reconcile their relationship. Of course, such a process is dependent on the victim truly offering forgiveness and recognizing the thoughts, feelings, and shared power of the offender; likewise, the offender must share power with the victim—a person who may feel that power was taken—and acknowledge the victim's thoughts and feelings as well. Thus, the process requires each person, the victim and the offender, to be *other-focused*.

But being other-focused is a challenge. The victim needs to feel confident that there will be no further betrayal. In addition, some ownership of how the betrayal had manifested may need to be addressed. For example, in a case of relationship infidelity, it seems easy to blame the individual who strayed in the relationship—but were there other factors that contributed to the infidelity, such as a lack of intimacy in the relationship? These are tough conversations because they can result in blaming the victim. Yet, many issues of conflict do not happen from a single moment but rather culminate from multiple, complex factors. Relationships are complicated.

With this being said, we need to be careful about attributing blame in any direction. A victim of abuse does not need to empower the offender, and forgoing feelings of trust and mutuality is understandable and perhaps even advisable. Principles of trust and mutuality cannot necessarily be applied to every situation.

The reality is that when it comes to forgiveness, sometimes we just can't "get over it." Maybe we are not ready to get over it and offer equal empowerment in a relationship. Or, perhaps the idea of acknowledging the other's thoughts and feelings is just too much! However, if the goal is reconciliation, a convergence of trust and mutuality is paramount to abandonment of negative feelings and the healing of relationships.

INTRAPERSONAL FORGIVENESS

In contrast to interpersonal forgiveness, intrapersonal forgiveness is an individual process that may occur on the part of a victim or perpetrator. In this process, re-establishing or reconciling the relationship is not always possible or warranted. Sometimes, relationships are unsafe, such as when one is abused in a relationship. This is certainly the case in our example with Sheila. We can understand the feelings of hurt and betrayal Sheila experiences toward her mother as well as her father. But can Sheila, or any victim for that matter, choose to let go of feelings of anger or resentment toward a perpetrator?

Think about a time when you felt like you were carrying around a lot of emotional baggage. How did you feel? Exhausted? Emotional? Depressed? Angry? Letting go of emotional baggage is tough, especially when the emotions are directed toward someone else. But maybe letting go of negative feelings toward others will be liberating, and this can increase a sense of emotional health and overall well-being.[11]

Perhaps the best way to think about why you might want to let go of emotional baggage is to consider the amount of energy it takes to maintain such feelings. Consider the following dialogue I had with a client who was harboring a lot of resentment toward her ex-husband.

> CLIENT: I removed myself from this relationship, but I'm still hurt. I'm so angry.
>
> RICK: If you felt like you were in a better place, what would that look like to you? How would you know you were doing better?
>
> CLIENT: I would not be so angry. But I'm just not ready to forgive him for what he did to me. For wasting my life with someone who never gave a shit about me!
>
> RICK: Being angry is important to you.
>
> CLIENT: It is.
>
> RICK: How about instead of trying to rid yourself of this anger you embrace it? You know, get up in the morning and spend the first 20 minutes of each day brooding about him and what he has done to you.
>
> CLIENT [laughing]: That seems a little counterproductive.
>
> RICK: It would take a lot of energy.
>
> CLIENT: Yeah, I can't see that as good for me.
>
> RICK: Me either.

Can you imagine spending considerable time focusing on negativity? The idea seems kind of ridiculous—to spend concentrated effort on being distressed. Undoubtedly, most people probably would never choose to do this, but when we hold onto resentment, this is what inevitably happens.

So, this leads us to the reason that intrapersonal forgiveness is such an important process. Looking again at Sheila. She may never reconcile with her father; her father may never change or even express remorse. In addition, Sheila may come to the realization that what she wants from her mother—understanding, compassion, and care—she is not going to get. And yet, should Sheila simply become accustomed to being angry? If Sheila is to live a healthy and productive life, does this include harboring anger, resentment, and frustration toward people who are unlikely to change or show the capacity of understanding, compassion, and care?

Probably not. Positive health and well-being would likely be described as overcoming the negative feelings that accompany any neglect or abuse. And because the offenders are not likely to be participants in this process, interpersonal forgiveness is not possible. Rather, the process of forgiveness is likely going to be an individual journey for Sheila—one in which she decides to no longer hold onto negative feelings toward those who have caused her harm.

But what motivates individuals to abandon anger and resentment toward others? Acknowledging the extent to which harboring anger and resentment affects personal wellness is an important consideration. After an individual recognizes the emotional toll that anger, sadness, resentment, and other negative feelings carries, an appreciation for an intrapersonal journey toward forgiveness might be understood.

Forgiveness can ease emotional distress. Let's face it: Letting go of anger and resentment is difficult. If it were easy, you would have likely chosen to do it a long time ago. But, where does it start? On an emotional level, you might be tired or frustrated dealing with the situation. It might be nice to start thinking, "I don't have to deal with this anymore." Stress is a major influence on health and well-being,[12] so there truly is benefit to ridding ourselves of this emotional baggage.

Forgiveness may seem like a relief from self-blame or self-doubt. A very serious obstacle in intrapersonal forgiveness can be self-doubt. Even when it is clear that you have been wronged, or victimized, guilt and self-blame can impede your progress—your ability to separate from an unhealthy relationship and move forward in life without anger or resentment.

Self-blame and guilt are normal feelings, particularly when one has been victimized. The process of working through self-blame and guilt can take a long time, and in these situations, intrapersonal forgiveness may not be at the forefront—nor should it be. At some point, however, considering how to move past pain and hurt and move forward from the harm of another may lead to a recognition that working through feelings of anger and resentment might be a healthier way to live.

UNDERSTANDING THE JOURNEY

Navigating through conflict and forgiveness is complex, and we can make it even more difficult by applying preconceived notions about forgiveness and holding ourselves accountable to unrealistic expectations. Regardless of whether an interpersonal or intrapersonal path is chosen, resist the idea that the decision is based on a particular trait or label. You are neither a forgiving person nor an unforgiving person; rather, how you perceive the situation may dictate what might be reasonable and helpful—both to others and yourself.

Interpersonal forgiveness is based on trust and mutuality, and it is difficult to conceive the renegotiation of a relationship if these attributes are not present. Intrapersonal forgiveness might provide the benefit of personal health and well-being, but there also needs to be a sense of comfort in abandoning hopes of a reconciled relationship. In other words, sometimes we have to accept that what we want from someone we are not going to get, so we need to consider

a path to move toward strength, peace, and well-being for ourselves without the presence of that relationship. Reconciling with
someone who has caused hurt or pain is not a mandate, but there are
both cultural and personal expectations that might make us feel like
we *should* renegotiate a relationship. We will discuss some of these
cultural expectations in Chapter 2.

NOTES

1. A Jewish tradition is to use G-d and omit the "o" in reference to the sacredness
    of the Name.
2. Balkin, R. S., Freeman, S. J., & Lyman, S. R. (2009, p. 154). Forgiveness, recon-
    ciliation, and mechila: Integrating the Jewish concept of forgiveness in to clin-
    ical practice. *Counseling and Values, 53,* 153–160. http://dx.doi.org/10.1002/
    j.2161-007X.2009.tb00121.x
3. Enright, R. D., Freedman, S., & Rique, J. (1998). The psychology of inter-
    personal forgiveness. In R. D. Enright & J. North (Eds.), *Exploring forgiveness*
    (pp. 46–62). Madison: University of Wisconsin Press.
4. Enright, R. D., & the Human Development Study Group. (1991). The moral
    development of forgiveness. In W. Kurtines & J. Gewirtz (Eds.), *Handbook of
    moral behavior and development* (Vol. 1, pp. 123–152). Hillsdale, NJ: Erlbaum.
5. Balkin et al., 2009.
6. Hall, J. H., & Fincham, F. D. (2005). Self-forgiveness: The step-child of for-
    giveness research. *Journal of Social and Clinical Psychology, 24,* 621–637.
7. Walton, E. (2005). Therapeutic forgiveness: Developing a model for
    empowering victims of sexual abuse. *Clinical Social Work Journal, 33,* 193–207.
8. Scobie, E. D., & Scobie, G. E. W. (1998). Damaging events: The perceived
    need for forgiveness. *Journal for the Theory of Social Behaviour, 28,* 373–401.
    http://dx.doi.org/10.1080/13557858.2012.655264
9. Khayat, R. (2013). *The education of a lifetime.* Oxford, MS: The Nautilus
    Publishing Company.
10. Jordan, J. V. (1991). The meaning of mutuality. In J. V. Jordan, A. G. Kaplan, J. B.
    Miller, I. P. Stiver, & J. L. Surrey (Eds.), *Women's growth in connection: Writing
    from the Stone Center* (pp. 81–96). New York: The Guilford Press.
11. Balkin et al., 2009.
12. Schneiderman, N., Ironson, G., & Siegel, S. D. (2005). Stress and
    health: Psychological, behavioral, and biological determinants. *Annual Review of
    Clinical Psychology, 1,* 607–628. doi:10.1146/annurev.clinpsy.1.102803.144141

Chapter 2

Forgiveness and Culture

Beliefs and Conflicts

Do we have an obligation to forgive? Needless to say, this is a rhetorical question, and you might be thinking, "Of course I don't have to forgive!" But then you might second-guess yourself. Why do we forgive?

Maybe we forgive because we are told that it is best. But in reality, forgiveness is more than just making the decision to forgive. In one study of 432 young adults, the decision to forgive was linked to increased stress.[1] Simply because you might make the decision to forgive does not mean you are ready for that process to take place. How often do people make relational decisions prematurely, whether it is about forgiveness or other types of relationships, such as marriage, divorce, leaving a job, and so forth?

Maybe we forgive because it is what is expected of us. In Sheila's story, her mother seemed to imply that forgiveness was a Christian mandate—*"You know as a Christian you have to forgive him."* And as we explore Sheila's situation, we can see how the mother's statement may have been more for her own benefit than Sheila's. Yet, there are times when culture and forgiveness are much more connected. Culture is often framed in terms of race and ethnicity but really includes a number of additional factors, such as socioeconomic status, religion, sexual orientation, gender, and language. Many religions focus on forgiveness as a form of righteousness. Other cultures might view forgiveness as a way of building peace between groups. So, as we reflect on the role of culture on forgiveness, culture should be viewed in terms of values, beliefs, and behaviors that are shared among people with similar worldviews, backgrounds, and histories.[2] Let's take a closer look at how culture and forgiveness may be interwoven.

AL SALAM MOSQUE, FORT SMITH, ARKANSAS, 2016

On October 2016, three men vandalized a mosque in Fort Smith, Arkansas. Of those three men, one of the men, Alexander Davis, wrote a sincere letter of apology while in jail. According to the *New York Times*, Davis admitted to the vandalism, causing pain to the Muslim community, being haunted by his actions, and being scared about his future. After receiving the letter by Davis, the Muslim community extended compassion beyond merely accepting his apology. According to the story in the *New York Times*, members of the mosque had just heard a sermon about the duty to forgive, and shortly thereafter received Davis's letter of apology. Upon receiving the letter, Dr. Louay Nassri, president of Al Salam Mosque, met with senior members of the mosque, and they reached out to Davis in an act of forgiveness. Nassri met with the prosecutor's office, indicated that the mosque wanted to drop charges, and opposed the felony charge on Davis. Davis was still charged with a felony despite the advocacy of Al Salam Mosque. The mosque paid Davis's fine for him, with a member of the mosque expressing to Davis, "I speak for the whole

Muslim community of Fort Smith. We love you and want you to be the best example in life. We don't hold grudges against anybody!"[3] Not only did members of Al Salam Mosque express and act on a duty to forgive, but also their actions demonstrated a commitment to this decision, as well as an emotional expression of forgiveness.

This is not to say that all individual expressions of forgiveness in a community are similar. There are distinctions between *emotional forgiveness*, the process of abandoning negative emotions and replacing them with positive feelings, and *decisional forgiveness*, which sees the offender as a "person with value," with the victim abandoning behaviors based on revenge or perhaps even restitution.[4] In decisional forgiveness, there is no reconciliation or interpersonal forgiveness, but rather just an intrapersonal process to abandon behaviors that could be perceived as vengeful, negative, or unhealthy. So, what we see in the Al Salam Mosque example is a community not only making the decision to forgive but also demonstrating emotional forgiveness in both their statements and actions. Again, it is important to emphasize that decisional and emotional forgiveness are two separate phenomena; they do not always occur together, if ever. One could forgo any type of retribution and even abandon any sense of fairness (i.e., decisional forgiveness) but not replace any negative feelings with compassion (i.e., emotional forgiveness). This would be consistent with intrapersonal forgiveness, in which a relational process is abandoned.

EMANUEL AFRICAN METHODIST EPISCOPAL CHURCH, CHARLESTON, SOUTH CAROLINA, 2015

On June 17, 2015, Dylann Roof entered Emanuel African Methodist Episcopal Church in Charleston, South Carolina during a Bible study and killed nine people, all African American, ages 26 to 87, with a handgun. On June 19, 2015, Chief Magistrate James B. Gosnell presided over the bond hearing of Dylann Roof. At the bond hearing, Dylann Roof appeared via video link, and family members of those who died spoke to the Chief Magistrate.

As reported in the *Boston Globe*[5] and the *Washington Post*, Felicia Sanders spoke about the pain of losing her daughter, Tywanza Sanders, and wished that "God have mercy on you." Representing the family of Rev. DePayne Middleton-Doctor, Bethane Middleton-Brown highlighted the nature of hate and a mandate to forgive: "We have no room for hate. We have to forgive. I pray God on your soul." Alana Simmons, a granddaughter of Daniel Simons, echoed the previous sentiments, saying, ". . . everyone's plea for your soul is proof they lived in love and their legacies will live in love, so hate won't win." Anthony Thompson spoke on behalf of the family of Myra Thompson, repeating the theme of forgiveness: "I forgive you. My family forgives you," imploring Dylann Roof to change spiritually. Nadine Collier, daughter of Ethel Lance, also repeated the theme of forgiveness: "You took something very precious from me. I will never talk to her again. I will never, ever hold her again. But I forgive you. And have mercy on your soul."

A variety of themes emanate from this court proceeding, which occurred only 2 days after the shooting—a wish for mercy on the soul of a mass murderer and white supremacist, Dylann Roof; the desire to forgo feelings of hate from the family members of the victims; and the desire to express forgiveness, perhaps voluntarily but also indicated as a mandate by some of the relatives of the shooting victims. Given the events that transpired and the near-immediate expression of forgiveness, one might wonder how the notion of forgiveness can be expressed, especially only 2 days after the family members were murdered. There was no demand for justice, but rather an expression to forgive based on faith, and perhaps a sincere belief that forgiveness is required. The decision to offer forgiveness came across from several family members of the victims, and therefore represented something beyond each individual affected by the loss of a loved one from the mass shooting.

There are some distinctions among Sheila's case, the Al Salam Mosque, and the Emanuel African Methodist Episcopal Church. Each of the assaults occurred at a different level. Sheila is dealing with an individual assault. Sheila was abused by her father, so this was an experience unique to her alone. The assault on the Al Salam Mosque was on a communal level. No individual was physically harmed; rather, a culture was singled out. The shooting at Emanuel African Methodist Episcopal Church was an assault at both the communal and individual levels. Dylann Roof was a white supremacist who specifically selected an African American church to attack the African American attendees. Individuals lost family members, and the community had to respond to a mass shooting initiated by Roof's racism and intolerance. So, when forgiveness is processed both individually and communally, each event must be viewed as a unique process, and culture may play a role in how each transgression is dealt with and viewed.

WE OFFER FORGIVENESS BECAUSE OF WHO WE ARE

One way to understand the connection between forgiveness and culture is to explore collectivism in light of forgiveness. *Collectivism* refers to how people view themselves in relationships with other members of their group; how people may be motivated by other members of a group; and how people may place more emphasis on collective goals rather than personal goals.[6] So, what we might often experience is that our beliefs and views about forgiveness are shaped by the people around us who adhere to similar values and belief systems.

Consider for a moment your beliefs about forgiveness—how do these beliefs reflect people in your group? Do you have similar beliefs about forgiveness as your parents or family? Do you turn to faith? Do you seek out elders? Or perhaps you turn to friends for advice or support, or even seek out counseling. As we saw in the cases described earlier in this chapter, religion is a good example of this.

Christianity has had an indelible influence on how forgiveness is conceptualized in Western civilization. Common elements found repeatedly concerning forgiveness and Christianity include dealing with hurt and anger, receiving G-d's forgiveness, emotional forgiveness, empathy, and reconciliation. Within the context of Christianity, members of the Christian faith identify with the brutal execution of Jesus, who nevertheless provides healing, regardless of the sin. Christian's view Jesus's execution as G-d's ultimate sacrifice to bring healing and reconciliation. Forgiveness, therefore, becomes one way of emulating Jesus. Recall that emotional forgiveness goes beyond the absence of negative feeling and also implies replacing the negative feelings with positive feelings. This high ideal may influence individuals to forgive, refrain from ill will, and even show mercy to a person who has committed significant transgressions toward others. However, reconciliation may not necessarily be viewed as integrated with the other components of forgiveness in Christianity. Reconciliation does not occur unless an individual has received G-d's forgiveness,[7] which places the statement, "May G-d have mercy on your soul," in a different context. In this light, a person who is not seeking change or showing remorse may not receive mercy. In Christianity, forgiveness is an act freely chosen.

Victims of an offense may turn to Christianity to pursue a process that may teach them to overcome or relinquish their negative reactions and to effectively remove them from the role of a victim.

The concepts discussed earlier related to Christianity and forgiveness are not unique to Christianity. Many of these ideas are shared among Eastern faiths. Hinduism, Buddhism, and Islam have similar conceptualizations of forgiveness and the propensity to forgive.[8]

In Hinduism, forgiveness is identified as one of the 10 virtues and is often referred to as *Ksama* or *Ksamata*, which translates to "compassion" or "mercy." Forgiveness is believed to be a sign of strength. The Indian spiritual and political leader, Mahatma Gandhi, indicated that the inability to forgive is associated with individuals who are weak. Forgiveness may be conceptualized as a mandate in Hinduism. The unwillingness to forgive and the ongoing presence of negative feelings or unresolved conflicts can be present in future lives.[9] But a primary difference between Hindu and Christian forgiveness may lie in the presence of consciousness. Christianity is tied to the belief that forgiveness is offered through faith in Jesus. With respect to Hinduism, forgiveness may be more immediate when one is conscious of transgressions and seeks peace and a renewed spirit, perhaps through such means as yoga or meditation.[10]

Similarly, Buddhism also explicates a conceptualization of forgiveness focused on consciousness and enlightenment. A tenet of Buddhism is rooted in Buddha's Four Noble Truths, which expound the notion that suffering is part of life. To be enlightened, we must move past feelings of anger or ill will toward others. Those who have committed transgressions should be viewed with sympathy and compassion. The pursuit of enlightenment leads to the elimination of pain and the proliferation of wisdom and mental fortitude.[11]

Islam and Judaism both indicate that forgiveness is not uncon-
ditional, which is in contrast to the previously mentioned faiths.
Islam is conceived as both a religion and a political entity, and therefore, matters such as forgiveness must permeate both daily living
and spirituality.[12] Within Islam, there are three aspects of forgiveness: waiving punishment, turning away from sin, and forgiving. But
for forgiveness to be granted, there must be the presence of contrition in the offender.[13] Hence, forgiveness is not a mandate, and if
forgiveness is not earned, then it is not necessarily given.

However, some interesting collectivistic differences were noted
between Jews and other faiths. Jews were more likely to identify
offenses that were unforgivable.[14] Traditional Jewish law delves into
how people are to manage harm, debt, and restitution. There are
many examples in the Hebrew Bible that indicate how harm, debt,
and restitution are handled (see Exodus and Leviticus), including
returning or replacing what was stolen or working off one's debt in
the event restitution cannot be made. In such instances, forgiveness is easy. Jewish law dictates how to make amends. For example,
I borrow your lawnmower, but as I am mowing my lawn I clum-
sily hit a rock and break your lawnmower. I get your lawnmower
repaired, and it works as well as it ever did. There is no problem.
I made appropriate restitution. I believe it is likely that you will
forgive me. But not all offenses that are viewed under the lens of
debt—an event in which an offender has caused some type of harm
or incurred a debt toward the victim—can be resolved through restitution. For some acts, there is no restitution. Acts such as slander
and abuse cannot be undone or set right. Restitution is not a viable
solution.

I use the following example with my counseling students: I am
giving a lecture. After the lecture, one of the students decides to
post on Facebook, "Dr. Balkin gave the worst lecture I ever heard!"

For some reason unknown to the social media universe, the post goes viral. Thirty thousand people respond with comments, emojis, and memes about my awfulness. The student realizes the error and removes the post and then comes to my office and apologizes. But what can be done? The information is already out there. Thirty thousand people or more saw that I was an awful professor. In this case, there is no restitution. The situation cannot be rectified, and it is incumbent on me to deal with that.

Such is the case with major transgressions, such as trauma, assault, abuse, infidelity, and neglect. Think about the cases we have looked at so far—Sheila, the Al Salam Mosque, and the Emanuel African Methodist Episcopal Church. In each of these cases, the offense goes beyond restitution. Both with Sheila and the Emanuel African Methodist Episcopal Church, there is physical harm: assault in the former, and murder in the latter. All three situations involve emotional trauma as well.

Similar to Christians, Jews believe that forgiveness on the part of the victim is freely chosen; only the victim can offer forgiveness. Jews are commanded to repent, but they are not mandated to forgive. Where Judaism deviates from Christianity is in the idea that forgiveness is generally a relational process between people.[15] To understand this and why this might be important, we can look at three terms that describe forgiveness in Judaism: *kappara, selicha,* and *mechila.*[16,17]

Kappara refers to spiritual cleansing. Judaism's holiest day of the year is Yom Kippur, the Day of Atonement. The holy day is devoted to fasting, reflection, prayer, and repentance. But liturgy is pretty clear that the Day of Atonement is a time to seek forgiveness from G-d and to improve on oneself. For transgression against another human being, Judaism requires that the offender reach out to the victim.

Selicha is likely the most accurate depiction of how forgiveness is conceptualized—a sincere willingness to abandon negative feelings toward an offender. Selicha is viewed as an act of mercy on the part of the victim toward the offender. And this may be all well and good if the victim wishes to reconcile with the offender, the victim is no longer in danger of future offenses or transgressions, and the offender has demonstrated remorse and changed behavior. But how does a victim move forward when these things have not occurred? Here, Judaism offers an answer.

Mechila refers to the forgiveness of debt, particularly a debt that cannot be repaid. In this situation, the victim recognizes that the offender will not repay the debt owed or that the debt owed cannot be repaid. This is the case with issues such as trauma, infidelity, and abuse. The act cannot be taken away, and what the victim would want from the offender is never going to be received. This is the case with Sheila and the love and security she may want from a parent that she is not likely to get. So, there is no reconciliation. Rather, there is only a recognition that holding onto such debt is not likely to be beneficial. In this situation, a victim may be on more of an intrapersonal journey with respect to dealing with forgiveness and conflict. We will talk about this process further in Chapter 3.

Up to this point, we have focused on religious identity with respect to forgiveness. Aside from religion, the historical antecedents of a culture play a major role in forgiveness. Let's take a closer look at the response from members of the Emanuel African Methodist Episcopal Church.

African American adults may be more likely to offer forgiveness and do so for religious reasons. Two national studies, each with a nationally representative sample of more than 1,000 adult participants, found that adults believed their capacity to forgive both others and themselves was enhanced by their participation in organized religion.[18] Sex differences were also evident among African Americans, with African American females more likely to offer forgiveness than males.[19] Forgiveness is more likely when the offender is not in a position to cause further harm,[20] such as the case with the shooter from Emanuel African Methodist Episcopal Church. The offender's incarceration might have had an impact on the victims' willingness to offer forgiveness.

The interaction with religion and culture plays an important role in developing a collectivistic culture that is more likely to seek understanding, forgive, and reconcile.[21] The relationship between forgiveness and religion among African Americans is complex. Reverend Solomon Iyobosa Omo-Osagie II of Baltimore City Community College linked the African American experience of slavery with "strong spiritual connectedness" that was essential for survival. The experience of slavery and the modern civil rights movement left an enduring mark among African American clergy who focus on infusing forgiveness with theology. Hence, the focus is not on hate but on healing. When the nation can atone for the sin of slavery, that atonement is not simply viewed as a way to find peace after tragedy and trauma but is also the tool to facilitate interracial healing.[22] In this sense, the Emanuel African Methodist Episcopal Church demonstrated the desire to forgive if atonement is demonstrated.

But beyond the spiritual connectedness with forgiveness, there is empirical evidence to support this path. In addition to forgiveness being linked to well-being, happiness, and improved mental health, forgiveness may be viewed as an essential component to intervening in the cycles of violence, counter-violence, and conflict within societies by promoting healing and reconciliation between groups, cultures, and societies. How does this happen? When a victim offers forgiveness to an offender, the victim may cease the actions for revenge and eventually let go of negative feelings, which enable the restoration of a relationship.[23]

In a survey of nearly 42,000 participants across 30 countries, forgiveness was ranked eighth in a set of 18 values that included the following:[24]

- Honesty
- Responsibility
- Love
- Open-mindedness
- Independence
- Courage
- Competence
- Forgiveness
- Intellect
- Self-control
- Helpfulness
- Ambition
- Joyfulness
- Cleanliness
- Politeness
- Rationality
- Creativity
- Obedience

But simply because those who are a part of a culture that abides by a collectivistic system can forgive does not mean they will. Barriers to this process include socioeconomic variables. The value of forgiveness appears to be ranked higher in countries with higher socioeconomic and quality-of-life indicators. Furthermore, people in countries that ranked higher in socioeconomic and quality-of-life indicators were more likely to indicate increased well-being.[25] People who are better able to meet their needs are more likely to forgive and experience improved well-being. Because this research focused on the socioeconomic indicators of a country and not on individuals of a particular social class within a country, the opportunity to forgive may be constrained by factors outside of issues related to a specific offense. When individuals cannot meet their needs, there is a systemic problem, and forgiveness may be less likely. Viewed in this context, we can understand why peace in the Middle East is so unattainable. The various factions have highly inequitable socioeconomic indicators, making forgiveness and reconciliation extremely difficult to achieve.

So, in a word, it matters where we come from. Your faith, your community, and your family all influence your perceptions, beliefs, and behaviors of forgiveness. Think about what you do when someone hurts you. Do you reach out to someone to help think things through? Do you seek counseling or someone to confide in? Maybe you turn toward your faith, practice meditation, or seek solace. Whether you look inward or reach outward to address such issues is less important than whether what you are doing works for you. At the core of addressing issues of conflict and forgiveness is this: Do you wish to be angry, hurt, or injured, or would there be some benefit in trying to get over this, whether you seek some interpersonal reconciliation or an intrapersonal recognition, consolation, and closure?

Now, make no mistake, there will be times that you might choose to remain angry. While we sometimes hear that it is always better to let things go (and we'll get to that momentarily), maybe a reason you choose not to let things go is that you might prefer to let them stay! Why would that be? There is power in anger.

Anger gets a bad rap. We tend to view anger as something bad that should be avoided or resolved, as opposed to a normal process. Even our media disparages anger. Think about *Star Wars*—anger is associated with the dark side of the force, and the Jedi should not give in to anger. When we watch a competitive athletic event, like tennis or soccer, we see athletes punished when they express emotion. But Kübler-Ross's classic model on grief and loss shows that anger is a natural part of the healing process.[26] We cannot merely accept the traumatic events that infringe on our lives; rather, we work through a process of denial, anger, bargaining, depression, and acceptance. Anger is real, and it is normal. As a matter of fact, you may even make fun of people who never seem to get angry. You might joke, "How does that not bother you?" Anger is temporary, but it is also where you are at a particular point in time. Sure, anger can be detrimental, leading to fighting, violence, and self-harm. But anger can also be constructive, and when channeled in a healthy way, it can lead to confrontation, change, and growth.

Anger is also viewed as a secondary emotion—a cover for feelings of vulnerability.[27] One of my mentors used to tell me a story about fox hunting. Now, I am not much for hunting, but I was always assured that they did not hunt the fox, but rather trapped it and set it free. Anyway, the group is on horses, and they chase the fox. The fox runs. Eventually, the hunters on the horses corner the fox. The fox turns to face the group, moves a front paw slightly back, and shows its canines. The fur on the back of the fox's neck rises. At first, the fox ran in fear. Then, the fox got angry and threatened to fight back. Anger is secondary to fear. So, maybe if you are dealing with anger, a thoughtful question to ask yourself is, "What am I afraid of?"

When dealing with angry feelings, particularly angry feelings toward someone, forgiveness may be furthest from your mind. From a collectivistic/cultural perspective, forgiveness may not be the answer. I was once asked during a workshop on forgiveness, "Should Jews forgive the Nazis for the Holocaust?" That's a hard one! Because we often think about forgiveness on an interpersonal level, people may find difficulty conceiving forgiveness toward a country or the individuals behind an abhorrently evil political movement. And yet, I have seen family members who survived the Holocaust make trips to Germany or Poland, tour the concentration camps, find family members and memorials, and come to grips with the past atrocities in a healthy way.

So, have I now convinced you that you should hold onto your anger or hurt, and not seek some type of interpersonal or intrapersonal process to forgiveness? Well, that is not my intent. What I would like for you to consider is that anger is normal. However, eventually dealing with that anger when you are ready, might be something you wish to consider. The research on forgiveness is overwhelming. And while we have focused on cultural aspects of forgiveness, because religion and culture have such an enduring impact on how a society deals with forgiveness, much of society is indeed secular. Many of the forgiveness concepts discussed previously, even those that are cultural or learned, have an impact on mental health. Numerous research studies linked forgiveness to increases in well-being, happiness, and mental health. A review of 54 studies on forgiveness interventions found that participants who receive specific interventions related to forgiveness experience increases in hope and decreases in anxiety, depression, and anger.[28]

We also see that individuals who have struggled through conflicts and have processed forgiveness report decreases in depression and stress.[29] For example, in a study of 674 African American men, the effects of everyday racial discrimination were linked to an increased presence of mental health distress; however, mental health distress decreased among participants who identified higher levels of forgiveness, and mental health distress increased among participants who identified lower levels of forgiveness.[30] The research points to a pretty clear trend. Even if, as discussed earlier, anger is a normal part of the process of working through conflicts, the advantages of working through issues of forgiveness appear to include meaningful mental health benefits.

WHEN CULTURE AND HEALING CONFLICT

So far, part of our focus has been on the role that culture plays in the forgiveness process. In the events surrounding both the Al Salam Mosque and Emanuel African Methodist Episcopal Church, the decision to forgive is based, in part, on faith and culture. Note however, that simply because decisional forgiveness is offered, it does not mean that emotional forgiveness naturally follows. Perceiving someone as having value and abandoning the desire for revenge (decisional forgiveness) is quite different from abandoning negative feelings and replacing them with positive feelings toward an offender (emotional forgiveness). But what about when our inclinations toward a situation or offender conflict with our religion or culture? Let's revisit Sheila's case. "You know as a Christian," Sheila's mother said, "you have to forgive him." There are many layers to this.

We can look at the unhealthy manipulation by the mother, which appears unsupportive and reflective of her own self-interest—keeping her family together and marriage intact—as opposed to the safety and well-being of her daughter. And the process used to meet those needs is to fall back on an ill-conceived religious mandate. Sheila is placed in an untenable situation—to compromise her own safety and well-being or to choose her own safety and well-being and abandon her family and faith. Of course, Sheila does not really have to abandon her faith but rather has to abandon her mother's deleterious interpretation of her faith.

Nevertheless, whether it is faith, family, or other external expectations, Sheila's story serves as an example of how individuals may be pressured to make decisions against their own self-interests. The influences of family, faith, and culture are enormous, and if even the norms of a family are contradictory to a healthy system of faith, such norms still shape us. Abuse and neglect often go unreported, and when they are reported, such circumstances have usually taken place over years. Rarely is the first instance of abuse reported. Rather, such situations are found out over long periods of time.[31]

Working through conflict and forgiveness, especially when such expectations emanate from one's culture, may require an openness to other interpretations and a reconsideration of the values endorsed by an immediate family system or community. This would be the case with Sheila. Not only does she have to envision her life without the parental support a teenager is accustomed to, but she may also have to reconcile her understanding of her faith and alternative interpretations to what her mother is expressing to her.

UNDERSTANDING YOUR JOURNEY

What are some takeaways from all of this—the stories on forgiveness, the cultural mandates, the emotions involved, and the decisions people make? Even when someone makes the decision to forgive, that does not mean the emotions involved with that decision are resolved. In fact, without addressing your emotions, and with only examining forgiveness as some cognitive, thoughtful decision undertaken to move forward, you might actually experience more distress. Mental health counselors refer to this as *cognitive dissonance*—the conflict between what you decide and how you are feeling. Imagine being forced to forgive someone? What would that look like? How would you feel?

I worked with a female, adult client who was abused by her brother. She indicated forgiving her brother because she had to— that this was some type of peace offering to keep the family together. Yet, she would cringe every time she came into contact with him. The discomfort never dissipated, and she resented how her family was able to compartmentalize their feelings and normalize their relationship with him at her expense. The reality was that her decision to forgive him was not real or genuine. She was still hurting and reliving the trauma every time she saw him. Eventually, she made the decision to separate herself from her family for her own well-being, realizing that the family was not going to change for her. That decision hurt, but finding a healthier support system, and reconciling that her family was not going to be part of her support system, eventually led to the development of a healthier sense of well-being.

The emotions you experience when dealing with issues of forgiveness, conflict, and reconciliation are normal. Taking time to understand your own feelings is an important consideration and can alleviate the stress when a decision to forgive is made. But, the decision to forgive does not necessarily mean the relationship is restored. Where people often struggle is with their anger—making the decision to forgive and then feeling guilty for still being angry or even wanting revenge. When these feelings are present, perhaps the decision to forgive is being rushed. In other words, we should resist viewing decisional forgiveness as a natural step toward emotional forgiveness. Just because you make the decision to forgive does not mean that you will naturally release all negative feelings toward the offender and replace them with positive attributes. The notion of emotional forgiveness might require believing that an offending person has value, but we should not assume that the action of valuing an individual will evolve into forgoing all negative feelings toward that individual.

We should understand that who we are is based on our culture, which is broad and complex. Culture includes many personal facets—ethnicity, religion, family, sex, gender, ability, and socioeconomic status, to name a few. Many of these facets are extremely important in our lives. Religion is a particular example where people turn for solace, comfort, support, knowledge, and answers. Our culture can be a viable source for rebuilding relationships and figuring out how to move forward. Other times, however, our culture can come into conflict with our own well-being. When this happens, we might need to turn to other resources or ways of understanding forgiveness.

Now, you may be wondering about why I spent so much more time discussing the Jewish conceptualization of forgiveness than I did other religions. And it's not just because I am Jewish, though we would be foolish to believe that my own identity does not play a role in how I conceptualize, research, and present forgiveness. The model that I present in Chapter 3 includes a Jewish conceptualization of forgiveness that I discussed in this chapter. You do not have to be Jewish to buy into this model. Rather, the concepts presented have some universality. From a scientific stance, this model can be generalized. From a more personal perspective, I think it resonates with people, and they find it useful. Let's have a look at it.

NOTES

1. Davis, D. E., Ho, M. Y., Griffin, B. J., Bell, C., Hook, J. N., Van Tongeren, D. R., . . . Westbrook, C. J. (2015). Forgiving the self and physical and mental health correlates: A meta-analytic review. *Journal of Counseling Psychology, 62,* 329–335. doi:10.1037/cou0000063

2. American Counseling Association. (2014). *ACA code of ethics*. Alexandria, VA: Author.
3. Tavernise, S. (2017, August 26). The two Americans. *The New York Times*. Retrieved from https://www.nytimes.com/interactive/2017/08/26/us/fort-smith-arkansas-mosque-vandalism-and-forgiveness.html
4. VanderWeele, T. J. (2018). Is forgiveness a public health issue? *American Journal of Public Health, 108*(2), 189–190. https://doi-org.umiss.idm.oclc.org/10.2105/AJPH.2017.304210
5. Associated Press. (2015, June 19). Families of victims deliver statements at Dylann Roof bond hearing. *Boston Globe*. Retrieved from https://www.bostonglobe.com/news/nation/2015/06/19/families-victims-deliver-statements-dylann-roof-bond-hearing/Yobn85Z4BTaMFnMhy8HQIJ/story.html
6. Hook, J. N., Worthington, E. L., Jr., Utsey, S. O., Davis, D. E., & Burnette, J. L. (2012). Collectivistic self-construal and forgiveness. *Counseling and Values, 57*, 109–124.
7. Walker, D. F., & Gorsuch, R. L. (2002). Forgiveness within the Big Five personality model. *Personality and Individual Differences, 32*, 1127–1137. doi:10.1016/S0191-8869(00)00185-9
8. Tripathi, A., & Mullet, E. (2010). Conceptualizations of forgiveness and forgivingness among Hindus. *International Journal for the Psychology of Religion, 20*(4), 255–266. https://doi-org.umiss.idm.oclc.org/10.1080/10508619.2010.507694
9. Ibid.
10. Hunter, A. (2007). Forgiveness: Hindu and Western perspectives. *Journal of Hindu-Christian Studies, 20*, Article 11. htpps://doi.org/10.7825/2164-6279.1386.
11. Menahem, S., & Love, M. (2013). Forgiveness in psychotherapy: The key to healing. *Journal of Clinical Psychology, 69*(8), 829–835. https://doi-org.umiss.idm.oclc.org/10.1002/jclp.22018
12. Mullet, E., & Azar, F. (2009). Apologies, repentance, and forgiveness: A Muslim-Christian comparison. *International Journal for the Psychology of Religion, 19*(4), 275–285. https://doi-org.umiss.idm.oclc.org/10.1080/10508610903146274
13. Rye, M. S., Pargament, K. I., Ali, M. A., Beck, G. L., Dorff, E. N., Hallisey, C., . . . Williams, J. G. (2000). Religious perspectives on forgiveness. In M. E. McCullough, K. I. Pargament, & C. E. Thoresen (Eds.), *Forgiveness: Theory, research, and practice* (pp. 17–40). New York: Guilford Press.
14. Cohen, A. B., Malka, A., Rozin, P., & Cherfas, L. (2006). Religion and unforgivable offenses. *Journal of Personality, 74*, 85–118. doi:10.1111/j.1467-6494.2005.00370.x
15. Ibid.

16. Balkin et al., 2009.
17. Blumenthal, D. R. (1998). Repentance and forgiveness. *Cross Currents, 48,* 75–82. doi:10.1300/J154v07n02_05
18. Wuthnow, R. (2000). How religious groups promote forgiving: A national study. *Journal for the Scientific Study of Religion, 39,* 125–139. http://dx.doi.org/10.1111/0021-8294.00011
19. Hammond, W. P., Banks, K. H., & Mattis, J. S. (2006). Masculinity ideology and forgiveness of racial discrimination among African American men: Direct and interactive relationships. *Sex Roles, 55,* 679–692. doi: 10.1007/s11199-006-9123-y
20. Ibid.
21. Hook et al., 2012.
22. Omo-Osagie II, S. I. (2007). "Their souls made the whole": Negro spirituals and lessons in healing and atonement. *Western Journal of Black Studies, 31*(2), 34–41.
23. Hanke, K., & Vauclair, C. M. (2016). Investigating the human value "forgiveness" across 30 countries: A cross-cultural, meta-analytical approach. *Cross-Cultural Research, 50,* 215–230. doi: 10.1177/1069397116641085
24. Ibid.
25. Ibid.
26. Kübler-Ross, E. (2005). *On grief and grieving: Finding the meaning of grief through the five stages of loss.* New York: Simon & Schuster.
27. Diamond, S. A. (1996). *Anger, madness and the daimonic.* Albany: State University of New York Press.
28. Wade, N. G., Kidwell, J. E. M., Hoyt, W. T., & Worthington Jr., E. L. (2014). Efficacy of psychotherapeutic interventions to promote forgiveness: A meta-analysis. *Journal of Consulting & Clinical Psychology, 82*(1), 154–170. doi: 10.1037/a0035268
29. Sternthal, M. J., Williams, D. R., Musick, M. A., & Buck, A. C. (2012). Religious practices, beliefs, and mental health: Variations across ethnicity. *Ethnicity & Health, 17,* 171–185.
30. Powell, W., Banks, K. H., & Mattis, J. S. (2017). Buried hatchets, marked locations: Forgiveness, everyday racial discrimination, and African American men's depressive symptomatology. *American Journal of Orthopsychiatry, 87,* 646–662. doi:10.1037/ort0000210
31. US Department of Justice. (2012). *National crime victimization survey, 2006–2010.* Retrieved on December 1, 2019, from https://www.bjs.gov/content/pub/pdf/vnrp0610.pdf

Chapter 3

The Forgiveness
Reconciliation Model

An Overview

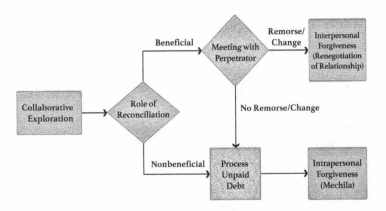

So far, a lot of emphasis in the previous two chapters focused on the role of forgiveness and the reasons that forgiveness can be difficult. And if you have bought into the concept that forgiveness, whether interpersonal or intrapersonal, can be healthier and perhaps even ideal for yourself or someone else, then the next question becomes, "How do we forgive?"

What often happens in mental health is that practitioners and researchers develop models. Models can provide a bit of "how to," but more important, they provide a way to conceptualize a process and develop a plan that has a reasonable chance of working for you. When I began to conceptualize the Forgiveness Reconciliation Model (FRM), Sheila's experiences were still on my mind. I can tell you that it had been about 4 years since I worked with Sheila. In that time, I completed my doctorate and was working in my first academic position. It was during Yom Kippur, the holiest day of the Jewish year, when Jews atone for their sins. I had attended morning services and decided to stay for a study session rather than go home, continue to fast, and stare at the refrigerator while I complained at how much my head and stomach hurt. The study group was well-attended, and the leader of the group led a discussion on the Jewish conceptualization of forgiveness, which I highlighted in Chapter 2. Recall that the following three types of forgiveness were presented:

- Spiritual cleansing (*kappara*)—the most spiritual and religious of terms
- Interpersonal forgiveness (*selicha*)—where the offender has demonstrated some remorse and change of behavior and the victim has abandoned negative feelings toward the offender
- The wiping away of debt (*mechila*)—based on the recognition that some debts cannot be repaid and that some apologies fall short of healing or even reconciling a relationship

It was the concept of mechila that most resonated with me. I immediately thought of my case with Sheila. How does Sheila begin to conceptualize forgiveness as it relates to her relationship with her father? I felt that the answer lied in this concept of mechila—for someone who has experienced abuse to be able to say at some point, "What I wanted from this person I am never going to get, so I am going quit expecting it. I am not owed anything. I'm just done."

To me this was such a powerful concept—the idea that one could release anger and ill will but not have the pressure of reconciling the relationship. Of course, it was contrary to what Sheila's mother wanted—for Sheila to forgive her father and for all of this to be swept under the rug. And it challenged my preconceived notions of forgiveness—that forgiveness was a relational process that involved some level of reconciliation with the person who committed an offense. With mechila, the victim was free to say, "You don't owe me anything anymore, but I do not have to have a relationship with you either."

As you read this, you might be thinking, "This concept is not new." You have probably heard or have had someone tell you, "I can forgive, but I cannot forget." But forgetting is not the same as holding onto anger or hurt or even wishing someone ill will. Even if you decide you no longer wish ill will toward someone, that does not mean you still do not feel hurt or anger.

Finally, as we begin to explore how we can get to this point of releasing feelings of resentment, hurt, or anger, I offer one additional thought. The idea of mechila—wiping away debt or seeking an intrapersonal path toward forgiveness—is only one possible conclusion. In some cases, reconciliation is possible; the idea of a relational process of forgiveness may be viable. Depending on the circumstance, working through a relational process of forgiveness and seeking to reconcile with the person who has caused hurt or harm may be beneficial. So, let's take a look at how one may work through this process and choose a path of interpersonal versus intrapersonal forgiveness.

FORGIVENESS AND IDENTITY: AM I A FORGIVING PERSON?

Famed psychologist Albert Ellis advanced the idea that we are all fallible human beings; people are neither good nor bad. Rather, we are what we do—and sometimes we do good things, and sometimes we do bad things. So, the idea of being a forgiving person is not so different, and in previous chapters, examples of how forgiveness may be influenced by context were discussed. For example, you might feel quite different if a stranger wrecked your car than if your family member caused the accident. Who commits an offense may be just as important as (if not more important than) the nature of the offense.

Or, perhaps individuals judge themselves as either forgiving or nonforgiving based on situations that seem very clear to them. For example, some individuals feel that regardless of the length of time in a committed relationship, if a person cheats in the relationship, the relationship should end. Others, however, may wish to devote time to trying to repair the relationship.

Yet, labels may be unrealistic and often are inaccurate. Particularly when it comes to mental health, the use of labels may be emphasized but often to the detriment of the person being treated. For example, diagnosis is not only a common practice in counseling but also is required in many cases. Yet, unlike other types of medical practice in which tests can be run and an accurate diagnosis identified, such practice in counseling is difficult to achieve. Documented attempts for psychiatrists to evaluate patients and agree on diagnoses have been highly illusive; psychiatrists are unable to identify consistent diagnoses and often are unable to agree with each other when seeing the same patients.[1] The point here is that consistent and accurate labels describing mental health are difficult and often inaccurate for the professionals who write the diagnostic criteria.

Moreover, the benefit of such labels may be highly questionable.[2] People who go to counseling are not likely to thank their therapist for their diagnosis. Curative factors in counseling are more related to the counseling relationship than a particular diagnostic label or treatment technique.[3,4] Even when a diagnosis is accurate, such a label rarely contributes to any meaningful progress in counseling.

What is the benefit, then, of reflecting on whether you are forgiving or unforgiving? The short answer is that there is not one. Such labels are not useful and should be avoided. The identification of such a label is not likely to result in any meaningful progress, interaction, or resolution, and the focus on such a label could inhibit progress or result in a lack of self-reflection or action toward any meaningful resolution. The decision of whether to forgive should not define a person or prescribe a label. Rather, an assessment of the situation—the context, the feelings, and the individual values— should be used to explore the forgiveness process. Forgiveness is a unique process in each situation, and the focus on using a general label to describe how all situations are handled is better avoided.

DO YOU HAVE A CHOICE?

The notion that forgiveness can be explored through an understanding of the context, feelings, values, and culture infers the freedom of choice. But choices, especially related to feelings, are not always clear. Do you wish to be angry, hurt, or injured? You probably have heard before, "Nobody makes you angry; you choose to be angry!" But is anger or hurt a choice?

You likely do not make a conscious choice to be happy in the moment; it just happens. The same is true for more adverse events. Think about what happens when we lose someone close to us. We might feel sad; we might grieve. And likely, the discomfort we are feeling is not a thoughtful response, but rather an automatic response to losing someone we cared about. Of course, there are times when we do have some control. You can probably recall moments when you thought, "If I think about it, I get sad, so I try not to think about it." We have all experienced events, both happy and sad, that when we take time to think about and put ourselves there in the moment, our feelings are affected.

So, we have some control over how we feel but not complete control. We can think about moments that make us feel happy or sad, and that might affect our current mood. But then there are moments that just happen to us, and our feelings are more like automatic reflexes. There is a name for this in the mental health field— *locus of control*—which refers to the extent that people feel they control their own destiny. Locus of control can be internal, in which individuals feel they are masters of their own destiny. Locus of control can also be external, in which individuals feel there are outside factors in control of what happens to them.

There are a lot of factors that contribute to locus of control, and it can be somewhat situational as well. You may experience situations, such as working hard at your job and getting promoted, for which you feel you controlled that part of your destiny. You may also experience situations in which you felt like you had no control, such as situations of abuse, neglect, or trauma.

Once again, the unique beliefs and perceptions about a given situation might differ according to the context of the situation, especially as it relates to feelings about the person who caused the harm. In a series of studies conducted with more than 700 participants in one study and more than 1,500 participants in an additional study, participants were randomly assigned a vignette, and their reactions related to forgiveness were assessed. Two important conclusions were noted:

1. We might be more inclined to forgive someone who is perceived as having less control of their behavior.
2. The victim's perception of the offender's control does not relieve the offender from responsibility. In other words, even if the offender engages in a behavior accidentally, the offender is still responsible.[5]

For example, consider the following story:

Rick is out on the road on his bicycle on a clear day, when suddenly he finds himself rolling on the ground. He attempts to stand up, but a severe pain suddenly shoots down his leg. He looks up and sees a white pickup truck pulling over on the side of the road. Another car pulls off the road, and a woman gets out, yelling, "Stay down! Stay down!" Confused and in pain, Rick realizes that he has been hit while on his bike. The energy drains from his body as the pain in his leg sets in. An ambulance can be heard in the distance. A woman is speaking to him, asking him for his name and anyone she needs to contact. He is able to tell her his wife's name and phone number. The ambulance arrives, and he is placed on a stretcher. A police officer arrives and tells Rick, "Quit moving your leg." Rick notices a man holding his hand. The man has tears in his eyes and says, "I did not see him." Rick is lifted into the ambulance. He hears a person say he that is starting a morphine drip.

Weeks after the accident, Rick is often awakened after a nightmare: the sound of broken glass after he is struck. When

Rick receives the police report, he learns he was struck in the back by the side mirror of a pickup truck. There is a moment of anger after reading the police report. No citation was given to the driver. Rick wants an explanation. The next day, he goes to the police station and asks to meet with the officer. For 24 hours, Rick has stewed with anger—"How could the driver not receive a citation?" The police officer comes out to greet Rick, and before Rick can say anything, the officer says, "Wow! Am I glad to see you! I was worried about you. Glad to see you are ok."

At this moment, Rick's anger dissipates. "How can I be mad at this guy?" The officer recalls the accident. "I kept telling you to quit moving your leg. You told me, 'I can't feel my leg,' and I was like, "Dude, I feel your leg. Quit moving it! I am so glad you are going to be okay!" Rick and the officer recall the driver who held his hand after the accident.

About 3 weeks after the accident occurred and when Rick is able to drive, he buys a six-pack of beer to bring to the driver's home to share a beer, thank him for stopping, and let him know he is alright. Unfortunately, the address is an apartment complex, and the apartment number is not on the police report. Rick wants to offer forgiveness, despite the traumatic event, but the opportunity to express the sentiment to the driver is simply not possible because there is no way to reach him. Even years later, the passing of cars when on his bike or in a car gives Rick chills. The residual effects of the trauma from the accident are present. Nevertheless, there is no ill will toward the driver.

Forgiveness likely came easy for Rick because he viewed the event as an accident. Although he is traumatized, even years later, he is not angry at the driver. In the face of the trauma, he is left with a distinct memory—one man, a complete stranger, tearfully gripping

Rick's hand. Rick remembers feeling genuine compassion and care from him, despite the pain in the moment. Within the trauma of the moment, there was a human connection.

The same cannot be said when a victim perceives that the offender has control over their behavior. Particularly when examining issues of abuse and neglect, there is a lack of the aforementioned attributes discussed previously—a lack of compassion and human connection when the infliction of pain and trauma is perceived as intentional. This would apply to Sheila's situation, suffering abuse from her father. When the forgiveness process is intrapersonal, devoid of the relational elements of interpersonal forgiveness, people may experience more difficulty. When the infliction of harm is purposeful, people may be less likely to forgive.[6]

Once again, consider what transpires for victims when an offender's behavior is intentional. The surviving family members of the church shooting at Emanuel African Methodist Episcopal Church, Holocaust survivors, and individuals like Sheila may eventually confront whether to pursue a path toward decisional forgiveness or emotional forgiveness. In the case of Emanuel African Methodist Episcopal Church, some of the surviving family members expressed decisional forgiveness, but not necessarily emotional forgiveness. Not only are these situations representative of an extremely violent event, but the recognition that the offenders are intentionally choosing a path toward violence is also pertinent.

Violent situations are not unique to the difficulty and conflict in addressing forgiveness. Breaches of trust may also influence the decision, particularly when trust was intentionally broken. Infidelity would be a prime example. When a spouse or partner chooses to cheat, the victim may have difficulty with learning to trust again and forgiving the offender. The complexity of forgiveness is in part driven by both the nature of the offense and the intent of the offender.

So far, we have explored the nature of control as it pertains to the victims' perceptions of whether the offenders were in control of their behavior. But we should also consider the extent to which a victim feels in control of their decision to forgive. Forgiveness, after all, is a decision offered by the victim.[7,8,9,10] When considering the context of the offense and the various types of forgiveness mentioned so far (e.g., decisional, emotional, interpersonal, intrapersonal), the navigation of forgiveness and the extent to which that includes reconciliation with an offender may be complex. Figuring out a pathway to guide the process of forgiveness may be helpful in abandoning negative feelings and moving toward a healthy disposition from an offense or traumatic event.[11]

THE FORGIVENESS RECONCILIATION MODEL

The process of forgiveness, whether interpersonal or intrapersonal, may be influenced by a number of factors, some of which we have discussed already. Context matters, as does the nature of the transgression and who commits the transgression. Your perception of the offender, the events, and your beliefs about forgiveness and reconciliation may dictate how you respond both emotionally and through your actions.[12,13] At the heart of the forgiveness process is the decision related to the extent to which the victim chooses an interpersonal process of forgiveness and renegotiates a relationship with the offender or chooses an intrapersonal path and accepts the fact that a relationship with the offender cannot be reconciled but that ill will toward the offender can be resolved.

The FRM, therefore, is a model that assists individuals in identifying the thoughts, feelings, and events related to the offender and the transgression and provides a pathway toward interpersonal or intrapersonal forgiveness. This is a process model, meaning that the central focus is on the process, not the outcome or endgame. As mentioned earlier, the goal with the FRM is not to define the individual as a forgiving or unforgiving person but rather to describe a process toward forgiveness that takes into consideration the uniqueness of each event. In other words, how one event is addressed with respect to forgiveness may be entirely different from how another event is managed.

The FRM is a four-step model that focuses on how one individual comes to the decision to engage in interpersonal forgiveness or intrapersonal forgiveness. Figure 3.1 provides a depiction of the FRM. Two alternate paths are presented—one leading to interpersonal forgiveness and the renegotiation of the relationship with the offender, and the other leading to mechila, the forgiveness of debt toward the offender and aligned with intrapersonal forgiveness.

The individual begins in an exploration phase, termed *collaborative exploration*. In this phase, the victim of an offense is encouraged

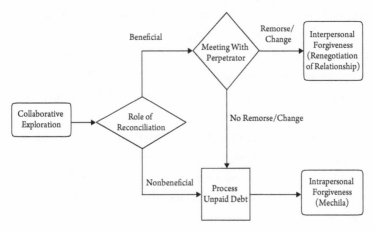

Figure 3.1. The Forgiveness Reconciliation Model.

to explore feelings toward the offender and the event. The collaborative portion of this initial phase is based on the idea that it is better to explore thoughts and feelings about the event and offender with someone—a person who is trusted—like a counselor, friend, or mentor. This is an opportunity not only to explore the trauma of an event and the feelings related to the event and the offender but also to explore feelings about forgiveness, such as asking yourself, "What do I think and how do I feel about the person who harmed me?" This is where your culture and worldview come in to play. In this process, you may have to ask yourself whether your worldview is in conflict with how you feel about the event and the offender.

The second phase is related to processing your beliefs about the *role of reconciliation*. After exploring your feelings about the event and the offender, you might want to consider your feelings about reconciliation and the extent to which you believe reconciling the relationship with the offender is beneficial or not. Some people may choose to do this individually, but talking this out with someone is likely helpful.[14] At the core of this phase is a decision, "What are the benefits and consequences of reconciling with the person who harmed me?" When making this decision, consider both personal well-being and personal perspective, such as how reconciliation fits into your beliefs held about forgiveness, whether personal, cultural, religious, or other influences. This is also a good place to explore any agreements or conflicts between personal well-being and deeply held beliefs about forgiveness.

Even if reconciliation is deemed beneficial, it does not always happen. The third phase, *remorse/change* refers to the offender's behavior. Does the offender express remorse and a willingness to change behavior? This process is external to the victim; the victim is not in control of this decision. So, when an offender does not show remorse or a willingness to change, reconciliation is not a viable solution, even if the victim believes reconciliation could be beneficial. This phase will likely dictate the future direction of the relationship between the victim and offender.[15]

In the final phase, victims are moving toward *forgiveness*, which can look like of one two alternatives:

1. Interpersonal forgiveness: an interpersonal process of forgiveness in which the victim and offender renegotiate their relationship; or

2. Mechila: an intrapersonal forgiveness process in which the victim recognizes that what is wanted from the offender will not or cannot be attained; the victim may wish to process the unpaid debt and release that debt, along with the emotional pain that accompanies the debt.

In summary, the FRM consists of a four-phase model: collaborative exploration, role of reconciliation, remorse/change, and forgiveness. Subsequent chapters will examine each of the phases in more depth.

ELEMENTS IN COMMON WITH OTHER MODELS

The FRM is unique in that it was based on a Jewish conceptualization of forgiveness. Throughout this conceptualization, forgiveness is a path that may be pursued interpersonally or intrapersonally. A victim can choose to engage in a relational process and negotiate reconciliation or work within oneself and remove feelings of anger or ill will toward the offender but not renegotiate a relationship. Hence, the decision to reconcile is to some extent at the crux of the model, but it is by no means a requirement. Forgiveness may occur with reconciliation or without—interpersonally or intrapersonally, respectively.

The fact that the FRM is based on a Jewish conceptualization of forgiveness does not necessarily reflect on Judaism from a position of faith of the victim. In other words, the FRM was inspired by a Judaic ethic, but being Jewish is by no means a requirement to work through this model. Rather, the concepts extended from Judaism are likely universal principles. In addition, with the notion of forgiveness being so grounded in culture and religion, this model is rooted both in principles of wellness and in ethical principles that have broad, transcultural applications. Accordingly, the FRM can be applied universally across a variety of cultures and circumstances.

Hopefully, the concepts of the FRM come across fluidly and with ease. Despite the unique aspects in the conceptualization of the FRM, the FRM does share common elements with other models. Here, we will look at commonalities and differences between the FRM and two other models from noted researchers in the area of forgiveness: Robert D. Enright and Everett Worthington.

Enright's model[16,17] is perhaps the most comprehensive model on forgiveness, consisting of 20 steps within four phases: *uncovering, decision, work,* and *outcome/deepening.* Both the FRM and Enright's model are process models. In other words, they both address courses of action toward forgiveness. Whereas Enright's model is a comprehensive model on how to forgive, the FRM is specific to how victims deal with others who have harmed them.

The *uncovering* phase is focused on the victim's emotional pain. Such pain usually manifests in hurt, anger, and personal consequences related to the offense or injury, such as shame, guilt, persistent anger, and health-related issues. Both the uncovering phase and collaborative exploration (the first phase in the FRM) require the individual to delve into exploring the events and the resulting harm from an offender, but the initial phase of the FRM places emphasis on exploration through a relational lens, which is addressed more in Chapter 4.

In the *decision* phase, the second phase in Enright's model, the victim identifies the consequences of unforgiveness—that feelings of anger or resentment toward the offender have not worked and that a personal change is necessary in order to heal. Hence, the victim makes the decision to forgive. This is where the FRM deviates from Enright's model. In the role of reconciliation phase of the FRM, the victim looks at benefits and consequences of reconciliation, setting up the extent to which forgiveness may be processed and whether it will be an interpersonal, relational interaction or an intrapersonal, individual experience.

Enright's *work* phase emphasizes the relational, interpersonal aspects of forgiveness. In this phase, the victim learns to accept pain and may even offer compassion and understanding to the offender. Again, the FRM deviates from Enright's model in that forgiveness is not always interpersonal. Furthermore, anger and hurt are valid; compassion and understanding can be difficult, especially when the offender has done little to be worthy of a victim's willingness to offer compassion and understanding. The relinquishing of feelings of anger and resentment, without necessarily offering compassion, may be sufficient. Others might suggest that this is not true forgiveness, but broadening one's definition of forgiveness and the relinquishing of anger can lead to less emotional burden and greater self-acceptance. This seems to be a viable form of forgiveness, but perhaps a form that is not traditionally viewed in terms of the interpersonal processes often emphasized.

In the final, *outcome/deepening* phase of Enright's model, the victim experiences the benefits of forgiveness—examining meaning and purpose from the journey, while releasing the burden from the offense and the offender. The release of burden is a similar construct in the final phase of the FRM, also identified as outcome. In the FRM, the final phase has two possible outcomes. One outcome recognizes a relational, interpersonal forgiveness between the offender and victim, in which a renegotiation of a relationship occurs. Or, an intrapersonal forgiveness experience incurs. Referred to as mechila, the victim releases the debt of the offender, relinquishing feelings of anger and/or ill-will. However, a relationship does not resume with the offender.

Everett Worthington developed the REACH model of forgiveness,[18] which has considerable research related to positive outcomes associated with the model.[19] The five phases share a number of commonalities with Enright's model and the FRM. The first step, *recall the hurt*, is aligned with collaborative exploration of the FRM and the uncovering phase of Enright's model. The second step is *empathizing with the offender*, which is consistent with Enright's third phase, work, in which the victim offers understanding and compassion to the offender. In the third step, *altruistic gift*, forgiveness is viewed as a selfless and compassionate endeavor from the victim to the offender, which aligns nicely with Enright's second phase of making the decision to forgive. The last two steps, *commit* and *hold onto forgiveness*, refer to the process of reminding why forgiveness was important and addressing self-doubts regarding the process. These steps align with Enright's final phase of recognizing the benefits of forgiveness. Clearly, there are a number of similarities among the three models discussed. However, there are some noted differences in terms of how forgiveness was conceptualized within the FRM and the sequence in which these models formulate the forgiveness process. Figure 3.2 highlights key similarities and differences.

Forgiveness Reconciliation Model	Enright Forgiveness Process Model	REACH Forgiveness of Others
Theoretical Framework		
Four phase model based on the Jewish conceptualization of forgiveness with a focus on managing conflict within the forgiveness process and culminating in a process focused on interpersonal or intrapersonal forgiveness.	20 step process model embedded in four phases on how to forgive and emphasizing a relational process between the victim and offender.	Five-step empirical model focused on a relational process to forgiving others.
Phases		
Collaborative Exploration: Exploration of thoughts and feelings toward the offender and event with a person who is trusted (e.g., counselor, friend, mentor).	**Uncovering:** Exploration of victim's emotional pain, anger, shame, guilt, and personal consequences related to the offense and/or offender.	**Recall the Hurt:** Coming to terms with the pain from the offender and making a decision to forgive and not pursue retribution.
Role of Reconciliation: An examination of the benefits and consequences of reconciliation, setting up the extent to how forgiveness can be processed interpersonally or intrapersonally.	**Decision:** Exploration of the consequences of not forgiving—feelings of anger or resentment that continue to affect the victim—and identifying that a personal change is necessary in order to heal.	**Empathizing with the Offender:** The victim offers understanding and compassion to the offender.
Remorse/Change: An evaluation of the offender's disposition—does the offender express remorse and a demonstrate a change in behavior?	**Work:** The victim learns to accept the pain from the offender and/or offense and may offer compassion and understanding toward the offender	**Altruistic Gift:** Forgiveness is offered as a selfless and compassionate endeavor from the victim to the offender
Outcome: The victim either initiates an interpersonal forgiveness process, in which the victim and offender renegotiate their relationship, or an intrapersonal forgiveness process, in which the victim releases feelings of ill-will, emotional pain, and the accompanying debt.	**Outcome/Deepening:** Victim examines meaning and purpose of their journey, while releasing burden of the offense from the offender. The victim experiences a release of emotional pain.	**Commitment and Hold on to Forgiveness:** Reminding oneself on the importance of forgiveness and addressing self-doubts about the process.

Figure 3.2. Highlights of key similarities and differences between the Forgiveness Reconciliation Model, Enright's model, and Worthington's model.

WHAT ABOUT SELF-FORGIVENESS?

Absent from the discussion so far has been consideration of self-forgiveness—how individuals negotiate through a forgiveness process when they are the offenders seeking forgiveness and reconciliation. Both Enright and Worthington addressed self-forgiveness in their models. Research on the FRM is limited to participants processing issues of conflict and forgiveness with an offender, and the FRM was developed specifically with this scenario in mind. However, the theory could be applied to self-forgiveness. Exploring the thoughts and feelings toward the victim, examining the benefits of reconciliation, and coming to terms with personal remorse and a demonstrated change in behavior could result in a renegotiated relationship with the victim or a resolution in which reconciliation with the victim is neither healthy nor possible. In the latter case, the offender might need to come to terms with the fact that some debts can be relieved but not repaid.

The importance of the second stage of the FRM, role of reconciliation, cannot be understated. Recall that it is in this phase that the benefits of reconciliation, or lack thereof, are processed. "Who does reconciliation benefit?" is a key question. Self-forgiveness has the potential to be an extremely selfish endeavor, particular when the benefits to the offender outweigh the benefits to the victim. Pursuing reconciliation with a victim, when the victim has not chosen this path, may result in continued offenses or retraumatization of the victim. Thoughtful consideration of the victim is key.

The failure to renegotiate a relationship should not necessarily be viewed as a failure in the forgiveness process. When an offender has demonstrated remorse, changed behavior, and exhausted the possibilities of reconciling the relationship, the concept of *mechila*, the release of one's debt, may need to be self-applied. At some point, an offender might have to come to terms with the idea that any compassion or reconciliation from the victim may not be given. There might not be another choice other than to accept this. On one hand, the victim is under no obligation to show any compassion or understanding to an offender. This is part of the offender's journey toward self-forgiveness—*"What I want from the person I hurt is not going to be given to me, so I am no longer going to expect it."* Processing this loss or inability to reconcile is part of the journey toward intrapersonal forgiveness.

UNDERSTANDING YOUR JOURNEY

The FRM and Enright's and Worthington's models are referred to as process models. In other words, they are used to guide individuals through a process of forgiveness. However, simply because the forgiveness process can be listed in finite phases (in the case of the FRM there are four distinct phases) does not mean that the work one engages in to process issues of conflict and forgiveness are easy. Simply put, forgiveness can be a difficult journey. I often remind my clients, "This can be hard. Be gentle with yourself."

The meaning behind the term *process model* indicates that the focus is on the journey, not the particular outcome. Notice that in the FRM, the final phase, outcome, has two possible endpoints: an interpersonal forgiveness or an intrapersonal forgiveness. This is a differentiation from other forgiveness models. People can find relief from anger, shame, guilt, or trauma in different ways, and sometimes those paths lead to a relational process; at other times, it might be best to find a way to accept the past and press forward in the absence of a reconciliation with the offender.

Regardless of the outcome of interpersonal or intrapersonal forgiveness, keep in mind that each process—each journey in forgiveness—may be unique. The goal here is not to diagnose or label oneself as a forgiving or an unforgiving person. Making the choice not to reconcile with an offender is not a bad outcome and can require as much strength and fortitude (if not more) as deciding to reconcile a relationship. Consider Sheila's situation, in which she does not return home with her mother who was unsupportive of the abuse allegations levied against Sheila's father. In many ways, it might have been easier for Sheila to backtrack and relent, but she realizes the danger this puts her in. Her journey in moving forward is a courageous choice, even if reconciliation does not occur.

However, in a completely different scenario, making the choice to reconcile can be beneficial and courageous as well. Consider couples who experience infidelity in their marriage or partnership and decide to seek counseling and renegotiate their relationship. Couples who never experience infidelity in their relationship are certainly worthy of admiration, but couples who stay together, despite obstacles and setbacks, are also strong couples.

What follows in subsequent chapters is a detailed explanation of each stage in the FRM. This will be followed by a method of evaluating where you are in the forgiveness process and understanding the journey ahead. When appropriate, actual data-driven support will be provided.

NOTES

1. Vanheule, S., Desmet, M., Meganck, R., Inslegers, R., Willemsen, J., De Schryver, M., & Devisch, I. (2014). Reliability in psychiatric diagnosis with the DSM: Old wine in new barrels. *Psychotherapy and Psychosomatics, 83,* 313–314. doi:10.1159/000358809

2. Kottler, J. A., & Balkin, R. S. (2017). *Relationships in counseling and the counselor's life.* Alexandria, VA: American Counseling Association.

3. Lambert, M. J. (Ed.) (2013). *Bergin and Garfield's handbook of psychotherapy and behavior change* (6th ed.). New York: Wiley.

4. Norcross, J. C., & Lambert, M. J. (2011). Psychotherapy relationships that work II. *Psychotherapy, 48*(1), 4–8. http://dx.doi.org/10.1037/a0022180

5. Martin, J. W., & Cushman, F. (2016). Why we forgive what can't be controlled. *Cognition, 147*, 133–143. doi: 10.1016/j.cognition.2015.11.008

6. Ibid.

7. Balkin et al., 2009.

8. Enright et al., 1998.

9. Enright et al., 1991.

10. Worthington, E. L., Jr., & Wade, N. G. (1999). The psychology of unforgiveness and forgiveness and implications for clinical practice. *Journal of Social and Clinical Psychology, 18*(4), 385–418. doi:10.1521/jscp.1999.18.4.385

11. Balkin et al., 2009.

12. Ibid.

13. Worthington & Wade, 1999.

14. Balkin, R. S., Perepiczka, M., Sowell, S. M., Cumi, K., & Gnilka, P. G. (2016). The Forgiveness-Reconciliation Model: An empirically supported process for humanistic counseling. *Journal of Humanistic Counseling, 55*, 55–65. doi:10.1002/johc.12024

15. Ibid.

16. Enright, R. D. (2001). *Forgiveness is a choice.* Washington, DC: American Psychological Association.

17. International Forgiveness Institute. (2015). *How to forgive.* Retrieved on December 23, 2018, from https://internationalforgiveness.com/need-to-forgive.htm

18. Worthington, E. (2018). *REACH forgiveness of others.* Retrieved on December 23, 2018, from http://www.evworthington-forgiveness.com/reach-forgiveness-of-others

19. Wade et al., 2014.

Collaborative Exploration

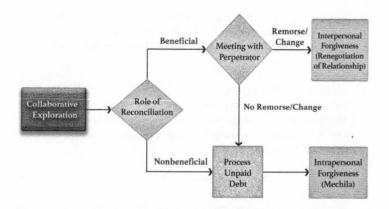

Having examined a process of forgiveness and how worldview and culture affect beliefs about forgiveness, the average individual facing pain, hurt, or anger toward another may not reflect on their own personal beliefs about forgiveness. Just like our feelings, which may be reflexive or at least secondary to how we think and the actions we take,[1] our thoughts may be automatic as well.[2,3,4] Now, that does not mean that our thoughts cannot be purposeful or changed, but rather that our thoughts can be more instantaneous. Let's consider some examples:

- Do you believe in G-d?
- Name someone you love.

- Do you think that abortion should be legal?
- Name someone in your life you dislike.
- Think of someone you cared about who hurt you.

You probably did not need to think too hard about these examples. For most of them, an answer, person, or idea quickly came to your mind. This is the nature of automatic thinking—and it was learned.

So, how do automatic thoughts play in to your feelings and beliefs about forgiveness? Your worldview about forgiveness was likely shaped by culture, family, and experiences you have endured. And for the most part, this worldview may have gone unchallenged. Certainly, people face events that shape their beliefs about the world around them, but day-to-day living does not compel us to change our worldview constantly. Of course, events happen in our lives that continually reshape us, but this often occurs gradually. Nevertheless, there are times when we face a crisis or event that reshapes how we feel about individuals in our lives. So, when we take the time to examine our own worldview, we should consider that this type of endeavor could represent a more introspective, personal journey, which is the initial stage of the Forgiveness Reconciliation Model (FRM)—*collaborative exploration.*

WHY IS IT COLLABORATIVE?

The initial stage of the FRM is similar to the initial stages in other models with respect to taking time to reflect on the harm or pain caused by someone. As mentioned previously, the initial stage of the FRM differs from other models in that the harm or pain caused by another is explored with a trusted person, such as a counselor, close family member, friend, or mentor. But why should feelings toward someone who has harmed you be processed with someone else?

My early clinical work was at an acute care psychiatric hospital on an adolescent unit where I led a survivor's focus group. The group members were generally adolescent girls and young adults 12 to 17 years old who had experienced physical and sexual abuse. For most of the members of the group, this was their first group therapy experience. As you might imagine, the first time they came to group was not easy. It was usually within a day or two from being admitted to the hospital, and often immediately after a traumatic event. At the initial group meeting, most patients refused to talk. I would gently try to encourage a patient to take a risk and participate. Quite often, the patient would be looking down, sometimes tearful, and would simply shake her head "no," declining the invitation. Sometimes, when a patient did decide to talk, it was often with some resistance or reluctance—"What is talking about this going to do?"

I think talking about a traumatic event does do something, when handled correctly. But the opposite is also true—processing traumatic events can worsen traumatic symptoms, particularly when treatment is brief.[5] However, in most cases, therapy can be helpful, and this brings us back to the initial risk that clients must take—to talk about their issue of trauma, pain, or conflict.

Pain can be so severe that it is easiest to avoid it—to avoid thinking about it, to avoid talking about it, to avoid reliving it. Particularly after a traumatic event, such as abuse, a person might be tearful and say, "I don't want to talk about it." To simply confront this behavior as avoidant is shortsighted at the least, and potentially harmful to the individual at the most. Rather, this is a form of self-protection, and we want to be careful about lowering peoples' instinct to protect themselves. That protection is there for a reason and should be honored. But what happens, eventually, is that in their own time, they will talk about it. This will generally occur when safety and trust are established. With the foundation of safety and trust in place, what was once so bad and unmanageable can become less severe and more manageable.

First, the idea that something is so bad, that it is too difficult to even talk about, may become more manageable as it becomes more mentionable. In other words, with being able to talk about an issue, the severity of the issue will decrease. Second, by talking about an issue with another person, you are able to gain perspective, sometimes simply by saying the words out loud. Processing issues from a solitary perspective is less effective. By talking out loud, you get out of your head and take the risk of hearing yourself, as well as lending the opportunity to get feedback.

The concept of *catharsis* extends back to Joseph Breuer, a colleague of Sigmund Freud, and refers to the emotional release of unconscious conflicts during therapy.[6] So, people may be prone to feel better by talking through conflicts. For example, along with leading the survivor's group, I also worked with adults who struggled with addiction, anger management, and engagement in antisocial behaviors. Physical altercations with parents, their family members, or even police officers were common.

In one particular group I was leading, one of the patients said, "My mother is a fucking bitch!" I looked to the patient—Derek, a 19-year-old young adult with a history of drug use, dealing, and physical altercations at home—and asked him what made him so angry toward his mom. He responded, "She's always in my business . . . telling me what to do!" I asked, "On a scale of 1 to 10, with a 1 being no problem at all and 10 being totally unmanageable, how would you rate the situation with your mom" "It's a 10," he quickly said.

Another group member chimed in—Deanna, a 26-year-old woman who was admitted after a suicide attempt. "A little over a year ago, I went through a nasty breakup with an ex-boyfriend. I had no job, and I continued to live with him. His drug use got really bad. We would smoke some pot together, and then one day he asked if I wanted to smoke some meth with him. I told him 'no.' So, he put it into my food he was cooking. I got really sick. When I went to go lie down he raped me. It got worse, and I eventually started doing meth with him. Then I started shooting up with him, and he continued to rape me. So, I'm an addict, and I've been raped by my ex repeatedly over the past year, and that is why I wanted to die."

The group was silent for a moment, and then another member of the group—James, a 22-year-old young adult, said, "I think that's a 10."

Derek followed up, "I changed my mind. Mine is a 4."

Not only was Derek able to hear himself, but he was also able to gain perspective and understand the severity, or lack thereof, of his situation. What was once unmanageable to Derek suddenly seemed manageable.

From Deanna's perspective, she had achieved a tremendous amount of growth in a short period of time. When she had entered the hospital through the emergency department after a suicide attempt, she felt tremendously hopeless. At her first session, she told her story to me and at that time expressed that she wanted to die. Yet, by the time she volunteered to disclose in group, she no longer felt that way. Rather, she was focused on her recovery, both from her drug abuse and from the abuse from her ex-boyfriend.

What changed from Deanna's initial session, when she went from attempting suicide and being admitted through the emergency department to disclosing in group the extent of her trauma as feedback to another patient who was clearly catastrophizing his situation? There were probably a few external factors, such as being admitted to a locked unit and being kept under 24-hour supervision by hospital staff. However, Deanna's decision to talk and confide in a counselor should not be overlooked.

In the cases of both Derek and Deanna, catharsis, or the release of emotion, is not simply a tantrum or venting of anger. It is controlled and thoughtful. The processing of events, thoughts, and feelings does not result in further agitation but rather in a willingness to disclose what is happening in their lives. Although neuroscientists have not been able to establish the science behind catharsis, it is a theoretical concept that has survived the tests of time. Despite the history of the concept and examples of how this process works, people often remain indifferent to talking about pain, harm, and conflict with a trusted confidant, mentor, or licensed counselor. Journaling can be another mechanism for attempting to explore feelings about an offender and beginning the forgiveness journey. However, there is a strong relationship between the initial stage of the FRM—the ability to explore collaboratively one's feelings about an offender with respect to a specific situation—and the final stage of the FRM, whether one chooses interpersonal or intrapersonal forgiveness.[7,8]

THE POWER OF RELATIONSHIPS

The willingness to disclose the details of an offense, the feelings toward an offender, and the pain or harm experienced are dependent on a safe, trusting, and caring relationship with another, whether a confidante, friend, mentor, or counselor. Edward S. Bordin provided a foundational framework referred to as the *working alliance*, which is typically conceptualized as the relationship one has with a counselor with respect to their interpersonal bond, work toward tasks, and achievement of outcomes.[9] In therapy, the working alliance is the strongest predictor of counseling outcomes.[10] There are so many facets to therapy, some of which include clinical interviews, psychosocial histories, problem checklists, standardized assessment, diagnosis, treatment planning, and actual therapy sessions. In addition, countless variables affect counseling outcomes, such as previous counseling experiences, the client's unique history, client motivation, the strategies and theories the counselors use when working with clients, and clients' sense of hopefulness. Yet, none of these aforementioned components predict the likelihood of success in counseling more than the working alliance between the client and counselor.[11,12,13] When counseling is successful, clients typically do not say, "Wow, that diagnosis was spot-on!" or "Thank you for documenting my goals in the treatment plan." Rather, clients are more likely to show appreciation for the relationship: "My counselor understood me." "I could finally talk about things that were really difficult for me."

Need further convincing? Let's move out of the realm of therapy for a moment. Nearly everyone has a favorite teacher. I begin each semester by asking my doctoral students to think about their favorite teacher. I pause for a moment. I want them to close their eyes and visualize this person. "Think about the reasons that this individual was one of your favorite teachers." When they have this person in mind, I ask the students to write down some of those qualities. Then we share them. Usually, the students' lists include the following qualities about their favorite teacher:

- Has a good sense of humor
- Holds high standards
- Takes time to get to know the student
- Is relatable

- Can explain difficult concepts in an engaging way
- Makes the material applicable to the real world

What is interesting is what is not on the list, such as behaviors attributed to good pedagogy:

- Writes the learning objective on the board each day
- Aligns exam questions with the curriculum
- Provides written feedback that is nonthreatening
- Uses project-based learning

These behaviors are not irrelevant or unimportant. They are just not behaviors that resonate. What people remember is how their favorite teacher made them feel. It really is about the relationship.

The initial stage of collaborative exploration sets the stage for the victim to engage with a counselor, mentor, or trusted friend and form a strong working alliance. This is necessary to develop comfort in talking about difficult issues. Finding someone to trust or believing you can trust a person is not always easy. At this point, seeking counseling may be very helpful to this process. When healing occurs, it often occurs through supportive relationships, thereby making collaborative exploration a formative stage in helping a victim move successfully through the subsequent stages of the FRM toward interpersonal or intrapersonal forgiveness.

OVERCOMING EMOTIONAL BARRIERS IN COLLABORATIVE EXPLORATION

For some people, identifying a person who is trustworthy, caring, and safe is easy. For others, careful thought and consideration may be undertaken to establish a relationship. However, after safety, trust, and care are established, the work can begin. Because forgiveness is primarily focused on a transgression between people, emphasis on feelings regarding the individual who caused harm is at the core of this stage. Previously, anger was addressed as both a normal and a secondary emotion to fear. Of course, you may genuinely feel angry without being fearful of the person who harmed you. Rather, the fear could be more tied to, "What happens if I am unable to get over this and move on?" This might mean uncovering the obstacles related to anger, such as the inability to accept the person who caused harm or the difficulty in re-establishing balance in life. Exploring some of these common emotional obstacles can be helpful.

Hostility. If anger is normal and secondary to fear, what is going on when we feel hostility toward someone who has caused pain or harm? Perhaps our hostile responses can best be framed as self-protection, and these responses are both involuntary and voluntary. In our brains, the amygdala controls our nervous system, processes facial responses, and even responds to smells. In addition to controlling our fear response, it also helps us learn from fear-inducing events. So, when we come across someone who has caused pain or harm, we have an involuntary biological response stemming from that experience. Our brain is going to signal, "danger, danger!" and that will likely manifest itself in our body language and facial expressions.[14] We might feel tense around this person. We could feel adrenalin. Our hands might tighten; our breathing might change; our heart rate might increase. To counter these effects, we might have to become mindful of what is going on with our body. Slowing our breathing and focusing on our body language, as well as how we verbally engage with the offender, might be considerations. Most important, there is nothing wrong with self-protection. When a hostile response toward someone is evident, consider that there is likely a good reason for the hostility. There is a benefit to this response because such a response can communicate wanting to be left alone or that the offender should be careful in their interactions. However, when hostile responses transfer to situations that would not otherwise warrant such a response, such as a panic attack in an environment that is generally non-threatening, that is cause for concern, and this is common in trauma. Feeling chills and stress when around an offender is normal, but when these reactions are transferred to other situations, there is probably some work that needs to be done in addressing the offense and feelings about the offender.

Aggression. When hostility is converted to action, aggression is the result. The hormone testosterone is released, increasing the likelihood of aggressive behaviors, including violence. Although males have higher levels of testosterone than females, females are more sensitive to the effects of testosterone. Thus, any evidence of differences between males and females may not be due to differences in testosterone. Furthermore, higher testosterone levels are correlated with aggressive behaviors, but not necessarily causal. There are other biological factors involved as well, such as serotonin, a neurotransmitter linked to depression. Lower levels of serotonin in individuals increase the likelihood of both aggression and depression.[15] The relevance here is that processing feelings toward an offender can be intense. When experiencing feelings of hostility or aggression, you might ask yourself, "What is wrong with me?" Understanding that these feelings are normal—even biologically based—can be helpful in recognizing the need to move forward, regardless of whether the eventual resolution is an interpersonal reconciliation or an intrapersonal outcome.

Exploitation. I worked with a husband and wife. He was a physician, and she was the clinic manager. Both were adept at their jobs. He had built a thriving practice, and she did an excellent job managing the billing and personnel. The only problem was that she hated her job. As she addressed this in counseling, her husband became quite irate, explaining that he needed her in the clinic. Eventually, I began to realize that she feared leaving the clinic because she was afraid he would divorce her. He was unwilling to be supportive of her finding another job. As she began to process that maybe she needed to leave to avoid feeling used, they quit coming to counseling. Hence, the type of pain that can be inflicted by an offender can be quite complex. In this example, the husband was extremely controlling in terms of removing support both emotionally and financially. She felt conflicted in her desire to not work with her husband and not be controlled by him, and the dependency she developed on him as a provider. Obviously, feeling controlled or used can be difficult to admit. We often feel that we are weak for entering these situations, and the pain inflicted is not physical, so the consequences are often overlooked. However, processing feelings of exploitation should not be discounted because this type of pain is detrimental to one's feelings of self-worth.

Abuse. For both Sheila and Deanna, overcoming abuse is paramount to their recovery. Initially, issues related to abuse were about safety, legal implications (e.g., arrests, removal from home, shelter placement, investigations), and processing feelings of shame, blame, and guilt. Eventually, these feelings may focus on the offender. Sometimes, the processing of feelings toward the offender places responsibility on the victim, such as when Sheila's mother says, "You know as a Christian you have to forgive him." Other times, the processing of feelings occurs in a healthy way and leads to addressing interpersonal or intrapersonal forgiveness.

Consider the aftermath of Sheila's case. Sheila leaves the hospital and moves in with her aunt and uncle on her mother's side of the family. Her mother remains out of the picture, and her father is convicted and serves time in prison. In the United States, sentences for rape and incest range from as little as 6 months (South Carolina) to 40 years (Wisconsin).[16] After 7 years, Sheila's father is released from prison. As Sheila enters her young adulthood, there are various family functions from her father's side of the family. Nieces and nephews are graduating; cousins are getting married; family reunions are planned. Although Sheila has no desire to reconcile with her father and has been more focused on an intrapersonal journey, she cannot avoid him if she chooses to attend these events. Collaborative exploration can help Sheila frame her frustrations. In this case, Sheila tells her therapist, "I don't want anything from him. I don't want to deal with him. But he's there, and I have to. It's as if there is this forced reconciliation. I will have him in my life whether I like it or not, unless I choose to completely disengage from that side of the family, which I don't want to do."

Hate. Nobel Laureate, author, peace advocate, and Holocaust survivor Ellie Wiesel said the following:

> The opposite of love is not hate, it's indifference. The opposite of art is not ugliness, it's indifference. The opposite of faith is not heresy, it's indifference. And the opposite of life is not death, it's indifference. Because of indifference, one dies before one actually dies. To be in the window and watch people being sent to concentration camps or being attacked in the street and do nothing, that's being dead.[17]

To hate someone may embolden the offender, because it speaks to the anger and hostility the victim still carries. In other words, the offender gains power by the victim carrying hate. Processing feelings of hate toward an offender will require victims to address the control the offender still has on their lives. Part of the goal of addressing conflict and forgiveness is to be rid of this control that is attributed to someone who caused pain and harm. So, if carrying feelings of hate is discouraged, then what? Here, Wiesel offers an intriguing response. Hate is not the worst thing a person can feel—it is indifference. Wiesel identified indifference as a death before death. Acknowledging that someone, no matter how painful, has had an effect on you is healthy. Better to hate than to be indifferent because pain is real. It is only natural to have an emotional response to the person who caused the pain. Consider the opposite situation— where someone has inflicted pain on another person, and the victim is in denial about this. We often see this scenario in abuse, where victims make excuses, defend the perpetrator, or even blame themselves. But when the burden of hate, anger, and hostility becomes too taxing or oppressive, there is value in collaboratively exploring these feelings to begin the process of defining what forgiveness might look like to you.

Dissatisfaction. The emotions discussed so far have been rather extreme. Failed relationships or disappointments are a common reason people cut themselves off from one another. Infidelity, ghosting, bullying, lying, and slandering are often the cause of relationships falling apart, and these issues are difficult to get over. But not all offenses are traumatic. Sometimes, we simply feel let down in our relationships, such as when someone did not live up to reasonable expectations. Maybe you are mad at your partner for failing to take out the trash, and for whatever reason, you just can't get past it!

Sometimes, it is simply that people grow apart over time, and people feel anger and resentment over the time invested in the relationship. Although these situations lack the impact of the majority of traumatic examples discussed, these issues are painful and can be difficult to resolve without exploring the feelings one has toward the individual who perpetrated the harm or broke the trust.

Collaborative exploration is the first step to understanding your worldview. Whether seeking counseling or talking to a friend or mentor, this initial stage of the FRM provides an opportunity to process how specific instances of conflict and forgiveness fit with how you see the world. For example, many people see forgiveness as an obligation, and this could be for a variety of reasons:

- Religion
- Obligation to family
- Keeping the peace
- This is what I was taught
- Believing I am somehow wrong if I do not forgive
- Believing I am a bad person if I do not forgive
- Feeling better physically or emotionally

Some of these examples (the first four) often have less to do with the feelings of the individual who experienced pain or harm and more to do with that person's beliefs, what was learned, or the need to fulfill some type of external expectation; while other examples (the fifth and sixth) put unnecessary shame or guilt on oneself if forgiveness is not offered. Only the last is internally driven, and it is important to consider that forgiveness is something we do for ourselves, not others. This is in contrast to other forgiveness models that offer a view of forgiveness as a gift to the offender, such as Worthington's REACH model[18] discussed in Chapter 3. However, Worthington is not alone in this view; another scholar, Rabbi David Blumenthal, when describing the Jewish conceptualization of forgiveness, indicated that letting go of resentment and negativity toward an offender is an act of mercy.[19] Hence, forgiveness can be an altruistic act. However, the problem with this depiction is that altruistic gifts and acts of mercy elicit the idea that despite pain and suffering, the victim should bestow some type of gesture toward the offender. When the eventual choice between the victim and offender is to reconcile their relationship, this gesture makes sense. But when a victim is trying to heal from the pain, harm, and suffering perpetrated by an offender, the idea of bestowing an altruistic gift or act of mercy toward the offender may at the very least feel unpalatable and at most place such an unreasonable expectation on the victim that healing and growth are discouraged. This is especially true when a victim chooses intrapersonal forgiveness as a resolution, as opposed to reconciling the relationship.

CHALLENGING UNIDIMENSIONAL VIEWS OF FORGIVENESS

In Chapter 2, we explored how culture may affect individuals' conceptualizations of forgiveness. Let's revisit the case of Sheila. We have interpreted her mother's statement, "You know as a Christian you have to forgive him," as an expression that focuses on her own needs as opposed to the needs of her daughter. However, Sheila was certainly influenced by her mother's words and behavior, as well as by the precepts of the Christian faith practiced in her home. As Sheila's mother appears focused on her life that is unraveling fairly quickly—her marriage, her relationships, her lifestyle, and her security—Sheila is dealing with a multitude of mixed messages, familial pressure, and severe trauma. But let's entertain the possibility that Sheila's mother also expressed a sincere religious and cultural belief to Sheila—that despite what appears to be a manipulative motive, forgiveness is viewed as an obligatory aspect of their faith. We use our culture to figure things out. Sheila's mom is using it to keep her family together. Even if her mother's message might be considered nefarious in Sheila's case, the recognition that people turn to faith, prayer, meditation, or elders to find answers regarding pain and conflict is well-established. But sometimes, preconceived notions of forgiveness are a source of intrapersonal conflict—conflict within oneself. What do you do when the answers you receive from your worldview don't mesh with what may be healthy for you? This seems to describe, in part, the conflict Sheila is facing. She is processing the ongoing trauma from her father who sexually abused her; she is feeling guilt over the dissolution of her family and her father's arrest; she is hurt by her mother's denial and lack of support and understanding; and she is fearful for her future. When Sheila's mother opens their initial session together with a declaration that Sheila is obligated to forgive her father, Sheila is confused by the statement, in addition to feeling hurt and disenfranchised from her mother, because she questions the veracity of the belief. As a Christian, is she obligated to forgive her father?

One of the questions I often ask my clients is, "Are you willing to re-examine your perspective of forgiveness?" Usually when we think about forgiveness, it is with the idea of interpersonal forgiveness—a relational, conciliatory response that seeks to alleviate conflict and reconcile a relationship. In other words, Sheila's belief about the obligation of forgiveness is that she should at some point express forgiveness to her father and attempt to heal the relationship. In this respect, forgiveness follows the concept of the *altruistic gift* indicated in the later stages of Worthington's model, which Sheila is nowhere near at this time. Sheila may benefit from a more intrapersonal journey, but generally intrapersonal forgiveness is not at the forefront of how forgiveness is traditionally envisioned. Yet, interpersonal forgiveness, as the traditional concept of how forgiveness is conceptualized, is at the very least impractical and at most unhealthy or even impossible.

Religion and culture often bring a range of expectations about behavior, obligations, and aspirations, as well as providing guidance, teachings, meaningful rituals, peace, and comfort. Yet, the obligations or cultural mandates may be unrealistic at times. For example, consider the cultural and religious contexts of grief and loss. In Judaism, a person mourning the death of an immediate loved one is to *sit Shiva*. Shiva is a 7-day mourning period during which the mourner does not work, generally stays home, and focuses on the loss of the loved one. Often, mirrors are covered so that the mourner is not concerned with personal appearance. The mourner may have visitors. A memorial candle generally burns for the 7 days of mourning. It is an intense period, but is it really practical that after the 7-day period, the mourner has sufficiently grieved? The ritual of mourning might bring comfort to some but could also be highly insufficient.

In addressing spirituality among African Americans, death may be viewed as part of G-d's divine plan for each person's life, as well as a loss to those left behind and also as a celebration for the deceased who has transitioned to a better life with G-d.[20] Yet, the obligation of celebrating a life may be complicated by the feelings of loss for those in mourning.

In Hindu culture, death is viewed as change, but not as an end to life. An intense grieving period lasts for 13 days, during which one refrains from work, religious activities, and social gatherings. Hinduism discourages excessive mourning because it is viewed as damaging to the departing soul. Once again, a person of faith can experience conflict between religious expectations and the overwhelming feelings of loss.

Grief and loss may be examples where religion, culture, and one's feelings of obligation can be in conflict with how an individual feels and even what may be best. When cultural and religious mandates or obligations come to the forefront of managing conflict and forgiveness, keeping in mind what is both practical and healthy is important. Religion and culture may emphasize a narrow or unidimensional view of forgiveness by only focusing on the more commonly conceptualized interpersonal forgiveness. But if interpersonal forgiveness does not represent a practical outcome because of, for example, concerns about safety of the victim or lack of remorse from the offender, then the victim may need to look at an alternative perspective to the unidimensional view of interpersonal forgiveness. For Sheila, if interpersonal forgiveness is a sincere, religious obligation, how does she move forward if reconciling with her father is impractical and perhaps even dangerous?

Looking for exceptions within culture and religion. One way to find relief from the feeling of obligation to reconcile with an offender and pursue interpersonal forgiveness is to look for exceptions. Steve De Shazer, a pioneer in the use of solution-focused brief therapy, highlighted that seeking exceptions can help reinforce the idea that some problems are not as persistent as we might perceive, and that alternative solutions are possible.[21] We do this quite a bit with religion and culture. For example, in Western religions, forgiveness is taught as a righteous behavior. Yet, no religion forces individuals to associate with people who do evil acts. So, an exception to reconciling with an offender, especially one who has not expressed remorse or changed his or her behavior, is forgiveness without reconciliation—intrapersonal forgiveness!

Cognitive rationalization. Rationalization is sometimes a dirty word. Renowned psychoanalytic pioneer, Sigmund Freud, identified *rationalization* as a defense mechanism, whereby unhealthy or contentious behaviors are explained logically, and the true ramifications of the behavior are avoided or denied.[22] But famed psychologist Albert Ellis used the term *rational beliefs* to describe the development of disputing distorted thinking and developing healthy beliefs.[23] Let's look at Deanna's case again. She considered her trauma from her addiction and abuse to be so severe that she should die. But at some point, Deanna rationalized that despite the severity of her trauma, her death should not be the outcome. Rather, she can figure out a way to persevere through this.

This may also be the case with Sheila, whose mother is using religion to encourage a reconciliation between Sheila and her father. Sheila must dispute the idea that she is obligated to reconcile. Rather, she might be able to dispute the religious mandate her mother is trying to force on her by considering that Christianity emphasizes forgiveness, but does not require reconciliation. Hence, Sheila then has the ability to redefine what forgiveness means to her and what forgiveness might look like.

Choosing you. Broadening perspective on views of forgiveness may begin simply by considering how a particular view of forgiveness is in the best interest of the person harmed. Or, if you are thinking about yourself, "How is my view of forgiveness helping me?" Sometimes, we cause more suffering to ourselves by refusing to abandon unhealthy belief systems or placing unreasonable expectations on ourselves. If Sheila believes that she must reconcile with her father, regardless of whether he has expressed remorse or changed in any substantial way, Sheila might be setting herself up for a dangerous situation or even for feeling like a failure in her inability to reconcile with her father and take care of herself. In the end, make yourself the priority.

UNDERSTANDING YOUR JOURNEY

The first phase of the FRM, collaborative exploration, is similar to other initial stages in forgiveness models in which the person who was harmed explores thoughts and feelings regarding the nature or circumstances of the offense. Where collaborative exploration differs from other models is on emphasis of two primary components:

1. A victim may focus on the feelings and thoughts about the person who caused harm. Coming to terms with the event is not the emphasis as much as coming to terms with the offender involved in the event. The FRM focuses on the relational components of forgiveness, which are best understood between two people as opposed to a person versus an event.
2. Collaborative exploration is a relational step, in which the victim is encouraged to talk to someone—a counselor, mentor, trusted friend, or confidante—about the nature of the offense and truly consider one's worldview about forgiveness and one's views about the offender. In collaborative exploration, the victim is going to have to take a risk—a risk to trust someone, to share a story, to gauge reactions, to process feelings, and possibly to challenge beliefs.

Eventually, an individual who has experienced conflict with another and feels wronged will have to decide on whether reconciliation with the offender is beneficial, whether the offender has sufficiently changed, and whether a renegotiated relationship is possible and healthy. Exploring feelings related to the offender is an important influence in choosing a path toward interpersonal or intrapersonal forgiveness.[24]

NOTES

1. Glasser, W. (1998). *Choice theory.* New York: HarperCollins Publishers.
2. Beck, A. T. (1972). *Depression: Causes and treatment.* Philadelphia: University of Pennsylvania Press.
3. Burns, D. D. (1980). *Feeling good: The new mood therapy.* New York: Morrow.
4. Burns, D. D. (1989). *The feeling good handbook: Using the new mood therapy in everyday life.* New York: William Morrow.
5. Shedler, J. (2018). Changing the topic does not change the facts. *Lancet, 5,* 539. http://dx.doi.org/10.1016/S2215-0366(18)30093-2
6. Breuer, J., & Freud, S. (2004). *Studies on hysteria.* New York: Penguin Books.
7. Balkin, R. S., Harris, N., Freeman, S. J., & Huntington, S. (2014). The Forgiveness Reconciliation Inventory: An instrument to process through issues of forgiveness and conflict. *Measurement and Evaluation in Counseling and Development, 47,* 3–13. doi:10.1177/0748175613497037
8. Balkin et al., 2016.
9. Bordin, E. S. (1979). The generalizability of the psychoanalytic concept of the working alliance. *Psychotherapy: Theory, Research & Practice, 16*(3), 252–260.
10. Kottler & Balkin, 2017.
11. Duncan, B. L. (2014). *On becoming a better therapist.* Washington, DC: American Psychological Association.
12. Kottler & Balkin, 2017.
13. Lambert, 2013.
14. Stangor, C., Jhangiani, R., Tarry, H. (2014). *Principles of social psychology.* Minneapolis: Open Textbook Library.
15. Ibid.
16. National District Attorney Association. (2019). *State criminal incest statutes.* Retrieved on January 5, 2019, from https://ndaa.org/
17. Sanoff, A. P. (1986, October 27). One must not forget. *U.S. News and World Report.*
18. Worthington, 2018.
19. Blumenthal, 1998.
20. Branch, W. T., Jr., Torke, A., & Brown-Haithco, R. C. (2006). The importance of spirituality in African-Americans' end-of-life experiences. *Journal of General Internal Medicine, 21,* 1203–1205.

21. de Shazer, S. (1985). *Keys to solutions in brief therapy*. New York: W. W. Norton.
22. Freud, S. (1998). *Case histories II*. London: Penguin UK.
23. Ellis, A. (1996). *Better, deeper, and more enduring brief therapy: The rational emotive behavior therapy approach*. Bristol, PA: Brunner/Mazel.
24. Balkin et al., 2016.

The Role of Reconciliation

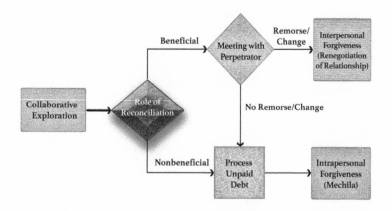

With an understanding of thoughts and feelings toward an offender through collaborative exploration, the second stage of the FRM involves a close examination of the role of reconciliation. Naturally, one might think that exploring thoughts and feelings a victim has toward an offender would inform how a victim perceives the role of reconciliation. But that is not always the case. When hurt, pain, and anger are involved, logical, rational thinking is not necessarily a given.

Consider the experiences of individuals involved in abusive relationships. Quite often, people who have suffered abuse continue to stay in a relationship that is clearly harmful to them. For example, nearly one-third of individuals arrested for a misdemeanor domestic violence charge were arrested again within 1 year, and nearly half of perpetrators were arrested again within 2 years.[1] Despite the fact that abusers have a high likelihood of abusing again, many victims remain in such relationships. Ending recurring domestic violence is not as simple as leaving the relationship: Upward of 70% of domestic violence victims experience abuse after separation.[2]

Lenore Walker's seminal work on domestic violence provided insight into the recurring nature of intimate partner violence and might be helpful for understanding the role that forgiveness plays in the cycle of abuse.[3] Walker noted a four-stage cycle. First, *tensions build*. Tensions can be very general and relate to anything such as alcohol and drug abuse, financial pressures, infidelity, relationship stress, and so forth. The stress in the relationship is followed by an *incident* of abuse and intimate partner violence, ranging from a variety of physical and emotional acts. The abuse is generally followed by an attempted *reconciliation* on the part of the abuser. The abuser will typically apologize, blame the victim, make excuses, and promise that the abuse will not happen again. The final stage is referred to as a *honeymoon stage*, in which the situation calms until tensions build again and the cycle repeats.

So, what might this have to do with the forgiveness process— the Forgiveness Reconciliation Model (FRM)—and the second stage of the FRM in particular? You might be thinking that all of this is specific to intimate partner violence. But that is not the case. The key point being made here is that in times of stress, pain, and hurt, making decisions that may seem in retrospect to be healthy, rational, and logical is not always easy, and even when such decisions are made, there can still be harmful repercussions, such as the recurrence of abuse even when separation has taken place. In addressing how to move forward after feelings of harm, pain, betrayal, or the breaking of trust, consider the role of reconciliation and the extent to which reconciliation would be beneficial in the forgiveness process.

THE RECONCILIATION DILEMMA

The extent to which reconciliation is an essential component of forgiveness is debatable and misunderstood. For example, Anglican and Roman Catholic clergy and the general population surveyed identified reconciliation as a pertinent aspect of forgiveness.[4] Perhaps we experience pressure from others to forgive and reconcile with someone who has caused harm. In Sheila's case, this pressure came from her mother. Or, we may put pressure on ourselves to reconcile, holding onto the idea that it would be better to not totally abandon the relationship we have with someone who caused pain. Part of the conflicting ideas over reconciliation stem from the various ideas held about forgiveness. The idea that forgiveness is "perceived to have meanings ranging from the forgetting of what has happened to the making of everything . . . as though it has never happened" still permeates today.[5] To suggest that a victim has the responsibility to *make everything* okay can contribute to revictimization. For example, Sheila's mother tells Sheila that she needs to reconcile with her father, but Sheila may be in danger if she follows her mother's request. Furthermore, the added cultural obligation from Sheila's mother, "You know as Christian you have to forgive him," places an unreasonable expectation on the victim, suggesting that for one to be whole, reconciliation with the perpetrator must occur.[6] Unfortunately, the belief that forgiveness is not complete unless reconciliation occurs has been stated in some professional literature.[7]

However, the notion that reconciliation is a requisite aspect of forgiveness is balanced by considerable research noting that reconciliation and forgiveness are separate processes. Going back to Enright's earlier research on forgiveness, a victim can move from anger, shame, and blame toward an offender to a healthier disposition without reconciling because the process of reconciling with the offender places the victim at serious risk for further harm.[8]

Existing research on reconciliation in the forgiveness process is quite ubiquitous in the professional and religious literature, and there is no real agreement about the role of reconciliation in the forgiveness process.[9] Honestly, this is not a simple issue; the relationship between forgiveness and reconciliation is multifaceted and involves cultural orientations (i.e., ethnic, religious, spiritual), perceptions about the offender, and the extent to which a victim is willing to consider that forgiveness can be an interpersonal or an intrapersonal process.

The challenge in this stage of the FRM is the personal reflection of how reconciliation is connected to forgiveness. In the case of Sheila, she is being pressured to forgive and reconcile, and perhaps these two components are viewed as one in the same. The dilemma is, therefore, *what happens if Sheila does not want to reconcile with her father?* Because reconciliation has been linked to forgiveness and her faith (i.e., "You know as a Christian you have to forgive him"), part of Sheila's healing comes from challenging her beliefs about the role of reconciliation in the forgiveness process. If Sheila is to be safe and heal, she will need to address her conflicting beliefs about reconciliation.

Notice the highlighted portion of the FRM at the beginning of the chapter. The second stage of the FRM, *role of reconciliation*, has two arrows emanating from it. The top arrow demonstrates a path that shows what might happen if the victim believes reconciliation with the offender is beneficial. The bottom arrow shows a path for when the victim believes reconciliation with the offender is not beneficial.

PROCESSING BELIEFS
ABOUT RECONCILIATION

Determining the benefits or consequences of reconciling with someone who has caused physical or emotional distress can be a daunting, emotional task. On the severe side, individuals struggling with issues of conflict and forgiveness might ask themselves, "How dead is this relationship?" When the choice to not reconcile is made, the relationship essentially ends. Ending a relationship with a coworker might not be that stressful. Ending a relationship with a significant other, family member, or longtime friend can feel like a punch to the gut or intense grief. In these situations, mourning over the loss of a relationship is normal. On the other hand, individuals might experience some relief when a relationship is terminated. Sometimes, the ending of a tumultuous relationship can bring about peace of mind ("I am glad that this is over").

In reality, beliefs and feelings about reconciliation are likely to be more conflicted—with a combination of both remorse and relief being experienced. We can think of this as a remorse–relief continuum, with an individual who is struggling with conflict and forgiveness being somewhere in the middle. One person may feel more remorse than relief about ending a relationship, whereas another may feel more relief than remorse, that is, less stress now that the relationship has ended.

Of course, sometimes people choose to reconcile and renegotiate a relationship with someone who has caused physical or emotional distress, even after experiencing harm from such an individual. Consider, for example, a couple who has experienced infidelity.

Jerome and Maria had been married for 13 years. Jerome served in the Army and had returned home after serving abroad in the Middle East. Maria worked as a vice president with a local bank. The couple had two children, 9 and 5 years old. Upon returning from active duty, Jerome admitted to his wife that he had an affair. They sought couple's counseling to see if their marriage could be saved. During the course of therapy, Jerome learned that Maria also had an affair while he was serving. As both individuals were troubled by the other's betrayal, reconciling the marriage seemed improbable. However, they both recognized that there were benefits to reconciliation, especially with regard to raising their kids and keeping the family together. They both admitted that their affair was not due to no longer being in love with each other, but rather about other issues—particularly loneliness, opportunity, and poor decisions. Ultimately, Jerome and Maria decided to continue in therapy and work on rebuilding their relationship, acknowledging more benefits in staying together and still caring for one another. They identified that strong couples are not necessarily perfect couples but rather couples who are able to work through their difficulties.

When one experiences some type of harm, emotional or physical, there may be a breach in the relationship. Of course, this is not always the case. Sometimes people experience harm, and the offender has no relationship with the victim, such as assault. Reconciling feelings about an offender when no relationship is present may be more straightforward. In the case where there was no relationship to begin with, then reconciliation is not an important factor, and an individual will likely work through the bottom portion of the FRM, as illustrated in the beginning of the chapter. But when conflict and relationships are more intertwined, reconciliation is much more complex. When the nature of an offense has caused a breach in the relationship, processing the role of reconciliation will inform further actions of forgiveness in later stages. Let's take a look at a way to process the role of reconciliation considering what it would be like to re-establish a relationship with the offender.

Constructive. The previous case of Jerome and Maria points to examples where reconciliation can be helpful. The couple decided they still have love for each other, and they reflected upon other factors that play into their relationship, such as raising their children together and keeping their family intact. The harm of the infidelity to the relationship appeared surmountable, with clear benefits to working things out. But these benefits are not considered as a distinct aspect of this stage. Rather, the benefits of reconciliation were informed by the initial stage of the FRM—collaborative exploration. Conceptualizing the role of reconciliation comes after thoughtful consideration of feelings regarding the person who caused harm. It is much more difficult to consider the role of reconciliation if feelings toward the offender are still raw or if the victim is unable to view the offender in any positive light.

Recall Sheila's father, who was abusive and served time in prison but was released. Sheila still has contact with her father's family and sees her father. But reconciliation with her father is uncomfortable, and perhaps even poses a danger. She becomes extremely stressed when she is in contact with him and does not view her relationship with him as beneficial. In this case, the initial stage of collaborative exploration informs the role of reconciliation—reconciliation is perceived as harmful, but avoiding the offender and associated triggers may be challenging.

Accommodating. One of the challenges in processing the role of reconciliation in a healthy way is related to the extent a victim wishes to be accommodating. A victim who reflects on positive feelings toward an offender in the collaborative exploration stage may be more likely to identify reconciliation as beneficial. But cultural views of forgiveness continue to have an impact on the role of reconciliation. For example, if forgiveness is viewed as an act of mercy that a victim extends toward an offender, then the motivation to view reconciliation as beneficial may be, in part, due to an effort to appear generous. The opposite may also be true. A victim may view reconciliation as beneficial in fear of appearing selfish. This could be the situation with Sheila. By Sheila's mother indicating, "You know as a Christian you have to forgive him," she applies both relational and cultural pressure on Sheila, in the hope that Sheila chooses to forgive her father and in turn keep the imaginary elements of her family together. Appearing selfish may have ramifications in the way Sheila is viewed by her mother, but sometimes selfishness can be viewed as self-care and self-preservation.

Other-focused. If Sheila feels shame or guilt for moving forward with the allegations, she may need to process her tendency to focus on others, rather than take care of herself. Engaging in behaviors that are more likely to appease others, rather than those that entail some type of intrinsic benefit, is a common experience. We all do things to maintain homoeostasis (i.e., balance). This is a common therapeutic principle. Change can be scary, and often people will act in ways to maintain the status quo rather than upset the balance and seek change. There is something scary about the unknown, and when change occurs, we do not know whether that change will be for the better or worse.

So, when someone who has been harmed is feeling pressure to extend forgiveness (as in the case of Sheila), even at the cost of individual well-being, such an act may appear selfless. But when the individual chooses self-protection, such behavior may be considered inconsiderate of others involved. For this reason, the extent to which reconciliation is viewed as other-focused, as opposed to looking out for oneself, should be considered. Keep in mind that this a not necessarily a right-versus-wrong answer. There are times to be other-focused, especially when reconciliation might bring about a common good and personal fulfillment, such as in the case of Jerome and Maria. But there are times when an individual who has been harmed by another really needs to look out for oneself, as in the case of Sheila.

Caring. Examining the extent to which reconciliation is beneficial is further complicated by feelings a victim may have toward an offender. Particularly when the cause of an offender's transgressions are due to trauma (e.g., post-traumatic stress disorder, or PTSD) or addiction, a victim may feel a sense of compassion toward the person who caused harm. For example, recall Derek, who is in recovery, has an anger problem, and was projecting his anger toward his mother. He might not seem like an ideal candidate for treatment. Yet, after hearing Deanna talk about her abuse and addiction related to her relationship with her ex-boyfriend, Derek was able to place his situation into perspective, admitting that he overmagnifies his problems, which feeds into his anger. For the average person in Derek's life, Derek may not seem like much of a redeemable person, but those that care about Derek might offer him some compassion, leading to forgiveness and reconciliation.

Some of the problems identified with the cycle of abuse point to instances where a victim has compassion for the abuser. Part of the control abusers have in the relationship is appearing vulnerable for a short period of time so that the victim feels compassion for the offender and opts to stay in the relationship. In many situations, however, this is not always the case. Abusers often attempt to exert power and control over the victim. Nevertheless, the previous referenced model of the cycle of abuse indicated a phase of reconciliation followed by a honeymoon period, which occurs because of manipulation from the abuser and often an attempt to elicit compassion from the victim.

Offering compassion to someone who has caused harm or pain is not necessarily a bad thing, especially if the offender has expressed remorse and demonstrated a change in behavior—a point of discussion in the next stage. The intention of offering compassion to the offender is based on the notion that reconciliation between the victim and offender is viewed as beneficial. The opposing circumstance is that the victim feels indifference toward the offender. This is not a problem if the victim understands that reconciliation is likely not beneficial and ultimately plans to pursue a more intrapersonal path of forgiveness. However, problems may occur if the victim is feeling pressure to reconcile but feels indifference toward an offender. This describes Sheila's situation. She is receiving pressure to offer compassion toward her mother and the breakup of the family, but feels fear and pain from what she experienced from her father. Addressing fear or indifference one feels toward an offender can be important for self-advocacy and maintaining safe boundaries.

Empathy. Another possibility is that a victim may feel empathy toward an offender. This differs from compassion in that the victim identifies feeling something similar to what the offender feels. Both Jerome and Maria cheated on one another. They likely both feel hurt and anger, but there is also an understanding of how vulnerable their marriage is, as well as an expressed desire to save their relationship. Perhaps the biggest danger to their relationship would be feelings of indifference—the idea that one simply does not care what happens to the other. Feelings of indifference are a powerful detractor to reconciliation, but sometimes such feelings are necessary to guard against a recurrence of abuse, especially when an offender denies problems and appears likely to reoffend.

Responsibility. Most people at some point experience some type of breach in a relationship. Sometimes, these breaches occur over small issues. Consider the following story:

> Robin and Jordan have lunch together fairly often, and they each take turns picking up the bill. Jordan begins to notice that every time it is Robin's turn to treat for lunch, they end up at a fairly cheap restaurant; whereas Jordan tends to select higher end restaurants. Tired of the inequity, Jordan begins declining lunch dates with Robin. Eventually, they see each other less often, and the relationship becomes far less meaningful, to the point that they no longer stay in touch.

Jordan felt taken advantage of, and subsequently felt that discontinuing a relationship with Robin was sensible. To continue in a relationship in which one feels taken advantage would be careless and would likely result in additional feelings of frustration or resentment. Although this seems like a rather minor issue, the vignette illustrates that people sometimes end relationships for fairly minor reasons. Issues of conflict and forgiveness do not always resonate around major issues or trauma.

But in the event that the issues are more serious, reconciliation can mean choosing a path that is more sensible or quite careless. Balkin and colleagues noted a common profile among women in domestic abuse shelters in which the participants in the study would identify that reconciliation with their abusive partner/

spouse would be careless, but they would proceed anyway.[10] Often, such decisions were influenced by other factors, such as staying together for kids or family, fear of financial hardship, or belief in the promises that the abuse would stop. Determining whether reconciliation is a sensible or careless endeavor may be clouded by personal biases—a preference for what is wanted versus the truth of the experience. Noted psychiatrist William Glasser used the analogy of a photo album to describe how people perceive what they want as opposed to what they really have, and one source of conflict is the distance between what is pictured in the album and what is actually transpiring, or how we want things to be versus how they really are.[11] For a person who experienced abuse from a partner or spouse, it is likely that the photo they wish to have is one of a satisfying, pleasurable relationship. Personal struggles persist when trying to reconcile the abuse incurred with the desire for a satisfying relationship. Glasser suggested that a source of emotional distress is based on the differences between what we picture and what we experience. The challenge, therefore, in evaluating the role of reconciliation is to identify differences between what is healthy, safe, and practical and what is potentially dangerous or harmful.

ARE FORGIVENESS AND RECONCILIATION A FREE PASS?

As the role of reconciliation is processed, the concern of whether forgiveness and reconciliation could lead to further transgressions from the offender toward the victim and how forgiveness and reconciliation might be experienced may be a concern. Notice that even in the definitions of forgiveness, the action is very one-sided. Both Enright[12] and Worthington[13] identified the victim offers compassion toward the offender; additionally, Blumenthal[14] conceptualized forgiveness as an act of mercy toward the offender. Clearly, there may not be much reciprocity in this process; it might even feel one-sided. Added to this is the nature of reconciliation, which goes beyond forgiveness. So, it's fair to ask, "Are forgiveness and reconciliation simply a free pass?"

Is Everything OK?

Fear of reconciliation is probably common. Most of what we know about reconciliation comes from couple's therapy, when there is distrust between partners because of such events as infidelity, deceit, addiction, or abuse. But a primary concern from the victim may be that forgiving and reconciling a relationship might suggest that "everything is ok." And if indeed an offender perceives that "everything is ok," the offender might be inclined to feel safer in the relationship and repeat the same behaviors that led to a breach in the relationship. In other words, "If I let my guard down and immerse myself back into this relationship, am I going to get hurt again?" This is a valid concern. After all, having been hurt by someone and then simply attempting to go back to the way things were seems inherently unfair. Self-protection is natural and normal. Sigmund Freud[15,16,17] devoted a significant amount of scholarly work, and a major contribution to psychotherapy, to defense mechanisms. He identified concepts such as *denial*, the extent to which individuals refrain from honest self-evaluation; *rationalization*, the tendency to explain away something that is problematic; and *projection*, the tendency to attribute your feelings on others. These defense mechanisms may inhibit personal growth and relationships, but they may also be a form of self-protection. So, when an individual feels defensive about offering forgiveness to someone, especially someone who has been harmful, then we need to be careful about challenging that defense mechanism because it may be there for self-protection. Exploring resistance and understanding the nature of a particular feeling can be helpful to making healthy decisions. Forgiveness can be scary, and it is okay to take time to consider the ramifications of forgiveness. Table 5.1 provides an overview of some defense mechanisms that might be common to issues of conflict and forgiveness.

A cursory look at the defense mechanisms in Table 5.1 might cause the reaction of, "Wow! These are not good qualities." And this is true to some extent. When we see or even experience denial, projection, displacement, and so forth, things are not going well. We are deceiving ourselves or attempting to deceive others, or others are attempting to deceive us! Still, it is important to consider not just the effect of a defense mechanism but also why it is there in the first place. Defense mechanisms are protective measures we employ to avoid hurt, pain, or discomfort. So, when you or someone else is defensive or resistant to change, take some time to consider the reason for the resistance.

Defense mechanisms may be an obstacle to reconciliation. Defense mechanisms may keep us safe. When recovering from a situation of hurt, pain, or abuse, being hesitant to accept reconciliation or that the offender is remorseful and changed may be a protective factor. The resistance to reconciling a relationship may simply be a message that (a) we are not ready to reconcile, (b) we are not sufficiently recovered from the hurt or pain related to the transgression, or (c) we are not ready to instill trust in the offender. Each of these is a solid reason not to pursue reconciliation, and our defense mechanisms may be a way to avoid reconciliation at this time. If, as Freud suggested, self-protection is innate—meaning that we

Table 5.1 COMMON DEFENSE MECHANISMS IN ISSUES OF CONFLICT
AND FORGIVENESS

Defense Mechanism	Definition	Example
Denial	Refusing to admit the presence of a problem, despite overwhelming evidence to the contrary	Refusing to admit being in an abusive relationship when there is overwhelming evidence of the abuse (e.g., physical assault, emotional abuse)
Projection	Thoughts, feelings, and behaviors about oneself that are unacceptable are attributed to another person	Being attracted to a person other than your partner but blaming your partner for attraction to another person
Rationalization	Manufacturing a reason to explain unhealthy behaviors	An offender logically explaining why an assault on another was justified
Displacement	Placing a feeling or action toward oneself on another object or person	Being angry at yourself and kicking the dog
Reaction formation	Assuming thoughts, feelings, and behaviors opposite of one's impulses	Having difficulty coming to terms with same-sex attraction and displaying aggressive behaviors toward LGBT individuals

Table 5.1 CONTINUED

Defense Mechanism	Definition	Example
Introjection	Accepting the standards of others to avoid negative perceptions from self or others	Assuming a subservient role in the relationship because of pressure from family or peers
Compensation	Attempting to cover a negative trait by consciously strengthening another trait	Compensating for having low self-confidence by being overly cooperative
Passive-aggressiveness	Indirectly expressing anger through passive behavior	Being angry toward a significant other but refusing to speak to that person

seek pleasure and avoid pain—then the idea that our resistance to reconciliation is healthy should not easily be dismissed. Defense mechanisms may simply be a *danger* or *warning* sign to proceed with caution or even to trust your own instincts at this time.

Defense mechanisms may leave open the possibility of reconciliation. On the other hand, there is the risk that the desire for reconciliation blinds an individual to the inherent risks associated with reconciliation. Stories of victims refusing to leave their abusers are all too common. The reasons for attempting to reconcile are varied. In a survey of 345 individuals (239 females, 106 males) who had been in abusive relationships, 14 common themes for staying in the relationship were noted:

- I would have been a failure if I left the relationship.
- I had no one to help me.
- I had to be the strong one in the relationship.
- I did not want to be perceived as weak.
- I was too embarrassed for someone to find out.
- I was too afraid of what he/she might do if I left.
- I had to stay to save him/her.
- I thought that the abuse was my fault.
- I had nowhere to go.
- It was not his/her fault that he/she hurt me.
- I had to stay to protect him/her.
- My religion would not allow me to leave.
- I believe marriage should last forever, no matter what.
- My children needed both parents.[18]

While some of these themes refer to the lack of resources or assistance (e.g., "I had nowhere to go") or the fear of retaliation (e.g., "I was too afraid of what he/she might do if I left"), other statements were indicative of the previously identified defense mechanisms, such as introjection (e.g., "I would have been a failure if I left the relationship;" "I did not want to be perceived as weak"); rationalization (e.g., "It was not his/her fault that he/she hurt me"); or reaction formation (e.g., "I had to stay to save him/her"). In the latter example, the impulse may be to leave an abusive relationship, but the decision to stay is based on the false presumption that the person can be "fixed" in some way and the victim then becomes the hero. Within these themes, we also see what is known as *cognitive distortions*—unhealthy beliefs such as self-blame or guilt (e.g., "I thought that the abuse was my fault"). Individuals who continue to feel responsible for the abuse they incurred may be at risk for putting themselves back in dangerous situations.[19]

An individual who has suffered harm from another may try to find ways to stay in the relationship. Leaving a relationship, even a bad one, can be a source of grief. Being hurt in a relationship can be traumatic, but being alone, especially when dependency was part of the relationship, may be extremely difficult. Recall Deanna who stayed in an abusive relationship with her ex-boyfriend, became addicted to crystal methamphetamine, and was raped repeatedly. Leaving the relationship seems like a simple decision, but aside from emotional or financial dependency, Deanna might feel like she can save her ex-boyfriend, believe that she is to blame for the abuse and failure in the relationship, fear being alone, or minimize the abuse incurred. Moreover, the offender might be reinforcing these beliefs because this is another way an abuser exerts control over the victim.

Premature reconciliation can cause blindness. Just kidding. But processing beliefs about reconciliation and the extent to which reconciliation is beneficial is important to addressing the questions, concerns, and potential resentment toward the offender. Obviously, a relationship that has been breached and in which the victim initiates a reconciliation process too soon can result in *premature reconciliation*—internal resentment from the victim toward the offender when forgiveness and reconciliation are pursued too soon—and may increase the likelihood of a permanently severed relationship.

Is this going to happen again? If a victim is living in fear or trepidation that the offender will commit another transgression, whether it is infidelity, emotional abuse, or neglectful behavior, then addressing that distrust is essential to reconciling a relationship. Of course, an offender who wants the reconciliation will often push back with, "How can I earn your trust if you do not give me the chance?" These tend to be circular arguments: "I do not trust you, and therefore it is too soon" versus "You will never trust me if you do not give me a chance." The risk in reconciliation is taken by the victim. Believing that reconciliation is beneficial and re-establishing a relationship with the offender place the victim in a vulnerable situation.

It's all normal. These aforementioned feelings and beliefs are normal and quite common to those who have suffered through abuse and abusive relationships. Defense mechanisms can play a positive role in preventing an ill-conceived reconciliation with an individual who is likely to inflict more harm. However, defense mechanisms also play a negative role in preventing relevant issues from coming to the forefront. Defense mechanisms may be a true impediment to reconciliation. Such an obstacle can be unhealthy if we need to deal with these issues or when we are unprepared to deal with issues regarding the offender. At the same time, defense mechanisms can be healthy if they are in place to prevent individuals from engaging in actions or behaviors that could be harmful.

Caution should be exercised when the victim is concerned about safety, either emotionally or physically. Abuse is often repeated, and many abusers commit abuse again with estimates as high as 65%.[20] But regardless of the situation or the severity of the offense, moving slowly should not be a problem. Reconciling a relationship should not feel like a high-pressure sell. When you feel defensive, that is a good signal to slow down and be thoughtful. Reflect on the defensiveness. Defense mechanisms tend to dissipate with comfort over a situation, and that is often a result of trust in a relationship.

Defense mechanisms may really be in the way. There are times when reconciliation is appropriate and healthy, and we would be remiss if we did not acknowledge this aspect of reconciliation. Knowing when to reconcile is important, and there may be times when moving forward and reconciling with an offender seems appropriate, but the victim remains resistant to the process. Once again, we can turn to the messages people often tell themselves when they encounter resistance:

1. *My defense mechanisms may be in place for self-protection.* We have addressed this, so let's look at the alternative.

2. *My defense mechanisms are unhealthy and an obstacle to my relationship.* This places the onus of reconciliation squarely on the victim. So, on one hand, the victim has been hurt by another, and on the other hand, the victim assumes ownership of reconciliation, which can come across as revictimization. Not only was the victim hurt in the relationship, but also the failure to reconcile the relationship is unfairly, and perhaps abusively, placed on the victim.

Working through resistance takes time. Rushing the reconciliation process can have ramifications both interpersonally and intrapersonally. Three influential factors to be considered, which appear in the forgiveness literature with respect to being ready to reconcile, are closeness, justice, and empowerment.

Closeness. The extent to which a victim identifies a connection to the offender matters. In Chapter 1, the following scenario was presented:

> An acquaintance who comes over to your house and takes something might never be welcome in your home again, but if a family member committed such an act, say a sibling, cousin, nephew, or niece, what would you do? Would you ban the family member if it were a single occurrence? Would you forgive the person if that person confessed and apologized?

Part of the context of what must be explored is the closeness between the victim and offender. Unfortunately, most of what is conjectured on closeness, as well as other factors, is based on hypothetical scenarios and college students as participants. College students may be more likely to forgive when their relationship with the offender is close, such as a family member or romantic partner.[21] One reason for this might be the perception of a shared value system. Often, people are close to others because they share similar beliefs and values. This is particularly important when the offender owns the offense. For example, an offender who cheats on a partner and values not only the person and relationship but also the importance of remaining exclusive in the relationship is more likely to be forgiven, with a higher potential for reconciliation in the relationship.

Power. The conceptualization of power in forgiveness and reconciliation has varying contexts. Seminal work in the areas of power and social influence identified six categories of power.[22,23]

- Coercive—uses threats of physical, psychological, emotional, political, or economic means to gain control or compliance
- Reward—provides or removes some type of tangible reward to enforce compliance
- Legitimate—enacts authority because that ability was granted through some process of social rules or norms (e.g., election)
- Expert—provides knowledge or skills in order to achieve or help others achieve a goal
- Referent—uses groups or organizations of which an individual belongs to enact a goal
- Informational—influences change through information

Power to forgive. Within these categories, the basis for power may either be taken by force (e.g., coercive), bestowed (e.g., legitimate), or earned (e.g., expert). With respect to forgiveness and reconciliation, the power to forgive can be based on any of these methods, and the type of power can fit each of the categories. For example, Jerome and Maria have the power to decide to what extent they want to forgive each other for their infidelity. This is likely to happen if they value their marriage and have a shared value system. In addition, they might be more likely to reconcile by each recognizing their own power to forgive the other. But let's assume for a moment that Jerome is having a difficult time forgiving Maria. He believes she was hypocritical to condemn him for his infidelity and not be transparent about her own. So, he is having difficulty getting past her deceit, not about the affair, but about condemning him without owning her behavior.

An innovative and important concept in relationships and power was identified by Willard Waller in 1938, known as the *principle of least interest*— the notion that the individual or group that has the least interest or investment in the relationship controls the relationship.[24] When the offender's desire to reconcile the relationship is more than the victim, the victim has additional power in the relationship—reward power! A victim may be more likely to express forgiveness when feeling empowered and when the victim feels that a sense of justice has taken place.[25,26]

Power to enact justice. Justice is often perceived as *what is fair* and thought of in terms of *retributive justice*—the extent to which a fair punishment has been administered.[27] But to what extent does justice lead to forgiveness?

When a victim insists on some form of retributive justice—a punishment to fit the crime—that seems almost the opposite of forgiveness. But punishment or retributive justice is not an exclusive form of justice. *Restorative justice* focuses on rehabilitation of the offender, in part, through an accountability and reconciliation process with the victim. Forgiveness is likely when any form of justice is administered but becomes even more likely when the victim has a voice in the process of justice, whether it is retributive or restorative.[28]

Power to have voice. These options of justice help, in part, to explain the process of forgiveness with the Al Salam Mosque and the Emanuel African Methodist Episcopal Church, which we explored in Chapter 2. With respect to the Al Salam Mosque, a restorative justice approach was taken in which one of the offenders demonstrated remorse and accountability and the Muslim community responded with forgiveness and advocacy. On the other hand, retributive justice was prominent with the victims of the Emanuel African Methodist Episcopal Church in which the murderer was confronted in court by some of the victims declaring themes of mercy and forgiveness.

Recall in Chapter 2 that we explored some of the cultural implications related to these events. But the dynamics of Al Salam Mosque and the Emanuel African Methodist Episcopal Church demonstrate the relevance of closeness, power, justice, and voice within the forgiveness and reconciliation process. Notice that revenge-seeking behavior is not identified with forgiveness and reconciliation. Revenge is often related to the victim lacking voice in the process of justice or to the system of justice falling short.[29] The victims from the Emanuel African Methodist Episcopal Church were given voice to the retributive justice process, which may lend to feelings of empowerment, especially when victims are unable to mete out justice.[30] Restorative justice may be effective because of the opportunity for the victim to lend voice to the process, hold the offender accountable, and be empowered to dictate the process of reconciliation.

UNDERSTANDING YOUR JOURNEY

The second stage of the FRM, role of reconciliation, is focused on understanding the extent to which reconciliation should be pursued within the forgiveness process. Conflicting ideas about the role of reconciliation within the forgiveness process exist; however, the FRM, as well as a significant amount of research, indicates that reconciliation should not be viewed as a mandate to successfully working through conflict and forgiveness. Instead, we focus on whether or not reconciliation is beneficial.

Processing feelings about reconciliation is important, but even feelings can be in conflict. For example, Jerome and Maria identified anger and hurt over each other's betrayal, but they also reflected on the positive aspects of their marriage and the desire to try to keep their family together. However, reconciliation is not always beneficial. The abuse Sheila incurred by her father or that Deanna experienced from her ex-boyfriend may be examples of when reconciliation is not beneficial.

So when is reconciliation beneficial? To answer this question, consider what it would be like to reconcile with the person who was harmful or hurtful. Beyond feelings for the offender—having care, compassion, and empathy—also consider the extent to which reconciliation would be responsible and healthy. There is a practical aspect to this process, and what may be envisioned may be idealistic and not practical. Looking back at Deanna's situation, what if Deanna attempted to reconcile with her ex-boyfriend? He was an addict who encouraged her drug use and abused her repeatedly.

Clearly, this is not a healthy relationship. But there are reasons that victims of abuse have difficulty leaving their abuser. Processing the role of reconciliation and emphasizing the healthy versus harmful consequences of reconciling are pertinent to Deanna's well-being.

A major challenge to processing the role of reconciliation is the extent to which defense mechanisms are present. If Deanna was in denial, for example, indicating that her ex did not really rape her or encourage her drug use—that she made her own decisions and he is suffering from addiction as well—she could end up making a very unhealthy and dangerous decision. Hence, it is important in this stage of the FRM to identify, understand, and work through defense mechanisms.

Defense mechanisms often are present as a way of self-protection. Sometimes, we are not ready to address issues. Sometimes, we simply need to slow down or proceed with caution. When addressing one's defenses, consider the following:

1. Get feedback. Whether it is a counselor or a trusted support person, an outside observer can be helpful.
2. Consider the extent to which what you envision matches what you experience. Sometimes, there is quite a difference between expectations and experiences, which can be a source of significant distress. Balancing the feelings we have toward the offense and the offender with the realities of our experiences can be important to a healthy process of addressing conflict and forgiveness.
3. Your closeness with the offender matters. Sometimes, reconciliation can feel like a forced process because escaping from the offender is difficult. An individual who was abused by a relative but never reported the offense may be in contact with the offender at family functions and have to manage these

situations. Forgiveness might even be less challenging when there is no proximity to the offender.

4. The extent to which you are willing or unwilling to forgive and to reconcile (keep in mind these are distinct processes) can be empowering, especially when the offender places more value on the relationship than you do. However, there might be times when the offender places no value on the relationship, which can be another source of pain and trauma.

5. Your ability to lend voice, and even dictate, the forgiveness process is another source of power. Reconciliation may be more likely when you are able to influence the consequences and provide a sense of justice. Sometimes, justice can be a severe consequence or punishment; at other times, justice can be a way for the offender to make amends. Both may influence your willingness to forgive and to reconcile.

Reconciliation is not always possible. And even if it is possible, reconciliation is not always beneficial. So far, the steps in addressing conflict and forgiveness have been internal—you have some control over taking the steps to explore your thoughts and feelings about the offender and consider your experiences and feelings related to reconciliation. The next step in the FRM focuses on an external process, in which there is less influence and control from the victim and in which much of the process lies with the offender.

NOTES

1. Puffett, N. K., & Gavin, C. (2004, April). *Predictors of program outcome and recidivism at the Bronx Misdemeanor Domestic Violence Court, Center for Court Innovation.* Retrieved on May 12, 2019, from https://www.courtinnovation.org/sites/default/files/predictorsbronxdv.pdf

2. Rakovec-Felser, Z. (2014). Domestic violence and abuse in intimate relationship from public health perspective. *Health Psychology Research, 2*(3), 62–67. doi:10.4081/hpr.2014.1821

3. Walker, L. E. (1979). *The battered woman.* New York: Harper & Row.

4. Macaskill, A. (2005). Defining forgiveness: Christian clergy and general population perspectives. *Journal of Personality, 73,* 1237–1266. https://doi-org.umiss.idm.oclc.org/10.1111/j.1467-6494.2005.00348.x

5. Ibid., p. 227.

6. Casey, K. L. (1998). Surviving abuse: Shame, anger, forgiveness. *Pastoral Psychology, 46,* 223–231.

7. Power, F. C. (1994). Commentary. *Human Development, 37,* 81–85.

8. Enright, R. D., & Zell, R. L. (1989). Problems encountered when we forgive one another. *Journal of Psychology and Christianity, 8*(1), 52–60.

9. Balkin et al., 2009.

10. Balkin et al., 2014.

11. Glasser, W., 1998.

12. Enright, R. D., 2001.

13. Worthington, E., 2018.

14. Blumenthal, D. R., 1998.

15. Freud, S. (1894). *The neuro-psychoses of defence.* SE, 3: 41–61.

16. Freud, S. (1896). *Further remarks on the neuro-psychoses of defence.* SE, 3: 157–185.

17. Freud, A. (1937). *The Ego and the mechanisms of defense.* London: Hogarth Press and Institute of Psycho-Analysis.

18. Eckstein, J. (2011, p. 25). Reasons for staying in intimately violent relationships: Comparisons of men and women and messages communicated to self and others. *Journal of Family Violence, 26*(1), 21–30. doi:10.1007/s10896-010-9338-0

19. Balkin et al., 2014.

20. Hamel, J. (2012). *Partner Abuse State of Knowledge Project: Findings at a glance.* Retrieved on December 1, 2019, from http://www.domesticviolenceresearch.org/pdf/FindingsAt-a-Glance.Nov.23.pdf

21. Wenzel, M., & Okimoto, T. G. (2010). How acts of forgiveness restore a sense of justice: Addressing status/power and value concerns raised by transgressions. *European Journal of Social Psychology, 40*(3), 401–417.

22. Raven, B. H., & French, J. (1959). *The bases of social power.* In D. Cartwright (Ed.), *Studies in social power* (pp. 150–167). Ann Arbor, MI: Institute for Social Research.

23. Raven, B. H. (1965). Social influence and power. In I. D. Steiner & M. Fishbein (Eds.), *Current studies in social psychology* (pp. 371–382). New York: Holt, Rinehart, Winston.

24. Waller, W. (1938). *The family, a dynamic interpretation.* New York: Dryden Press.

25. Wenzel & Okimoto, 2010.

26. Wenzel, M., & Okimoto, T. G. (2012). The varying meaning of forgiveness: Relationship closeness moderates how forgiveness affects feelings of justice. *European Journal of Social Psychology, 42*(4), 420–431. doi:10.1002/ejsp.1850

27. Strelan, P., Feather, N., & McKee, I. (2011). Retributive and inclusive justice goals and forgiveness: The influence of motivational values. *Social Justice Research, 24*(2), 126–142. https://doi-org.umiss.idm.oclc.org/10.1007/s11211-011-0132-9

28. Strelan, P., Di Fiore, C., & Prooijen, J. V. (2017). The empowering effect of punishment on forgiveness. *European Journal of Social Psychology, 47*(4), 472–487. https://doi-org.umiss.idm.oclc.org/10.1002/ejsp.2254

29. Aquino, K., Tripp, T. M., & Bies, R. J. (2007). "Getting even or moving on? Power, procedural justice, and types of offense as predictors of revenge, forgiveness, reconciliation, and avoidance in organizations": Correction to Aquino, Tripp, and Bies (2006). *Journal of Applied Psychology, 92*(1), 80. doi:10.1037/0021-9010.92.1.80

30. Strelan et al., 2017.

Chapter 6

Remorse and Change

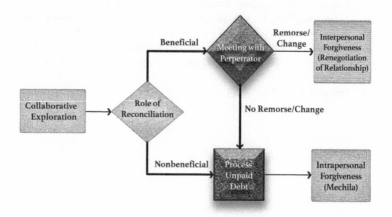

Addressing conflict and forgiveness within the Forgiveness Reconciliation Model (FRM) has focused on internal processes— the reflection of the victim on the offender and the circumstances, emotions, and practicality of moving forward with or without the offender. If reconciliation is beneficial, what do the next steps of in-terpersonal forgiveness look like? If reconciliation is not beneficial, how does the victim work through a process of intrapersonal for-giveness? To discern the path for the next steps in this journey, we will turn our attention to the third phase of the FRM—the remorse and change of the offender, which is an external process.

In the third phase, the victim's ability to dictate what happens is much more limited. Deanna, who struggled with addiction and was abused by her ex-boyfriend, cannot control whether her ex has remorse and will change his behavior. This is much different than the previous two phases, in which the victim could dictate the means of exploring thoughts and feelings about the offender and the offense and the extent to which reconciliation may or may not be beneficial.

Recall in Chapter 3 that *locus of control* was introduced. Locus of control refers to the amount of control that you feel over your own destiny. Locus of control can be internal, in which you feel you are the master of your own destiny, or locus of control can be external, in which you feel there are outside factors in control. So, internal locus of control may have been predominant in the first two phases of the FRM, but external locus of control is the predominant disposition for the remorse and change of the offender.

TWO ALTERNATE PATHS

The FRM illustrates two alternative paths. Both paths begin with collaborative exploration, in which a person explores feelings and beliefs about the offense, the offender, and one's personal worldview of forgiveness. The role of reconciliation is processed, and a decision is made as to whether there is benefit for the victim in reconciling with the offender. The point is essentially this: A victim cannot dictate whether an offender is going to be remorseful and change behavior. So, even when a victim explores feelings about the nature of the offense and the offender and sees the role of reconciliation as beneficial, that does not lead necessarily to a reconciled relationship.

Why is this? One consideration is that the extent to which an offender demonstrates remorse or change may already be determined or may still need to be determined. When reconciliation is deemed to be beneficial, a determination of well-being, and even safety, needs to be made. How should this be determined? At some point, if a victim is considering reconciliation with an offender, a meeting with the offender needs to transpire.

THE HEROIC JOURNEY

Meeting with the perpetrator, as depicted in the FRM, can involve a lot of emotions, fear, anger, depression, and anxiety. There is something extremely fearful about confronting an individual who has caused harm. This stress may be manifested in the idea that approaching or confronting an offender could set oneself up to be revictimized. We have numerous examples in which victims came forward, and the validity of the victim's story or allegation was called in to question by the perpetrator or other authorities, legal or otherwise. These stories are all too common among cases of physical and sexual abuse.

Carl Jung advanced the ideas of *archetypes*—that humans tend to identify images and ideas that have universal representations. These ideas and images come across in our conscious and unconscious behaviors (e.g., stories of redemption, good vs. evil, dreams). Archetypes are important to understanding a journey.[1]

Reconciliation and Redemption

We love our stories of redemption, whether the story is from a Greek legend, modern movie, or people who overcome adversity.

Take, for example, the story of Heracles. He was the son of Zeus and Alcmene. But Zeus's goddess wife, Hera, did not take kindly to Zeus's infidelity and cursed Heracles. Hera caused Heracles to go mad, and he murdered his wife, Megara, as well as his two children—a son and daughter. Part of Heracles's journey was redemption and proving himself a hero so that he could join the Olympian gods and goddesses.

Too far back for you? How about the *Star Wars* saga? If you have seen the movies (spoiler alert, so skip this paragraph if you do not want to know), Darth Vader is the evil father of the hero, Luke Skywalker. Darth Vader has done a lot of bad things, such as killing babies and blowing up a planet. But Luke senses good in him, and in one final act of redemption, Darth Vader kills the evil emperor, saving his son and the rest of the galaxy.

Need something real? How about Tiger Woods, who won his 15th major professional tournament after 11 years of not winning at this level. In that time, he was treated for addiction, had multiple surgeries, and had lost millions of dollars in sponsorship. When he finally won again in 2019, he was treated, not as someone whose wife divorced him because of multiple infidelities, but as an individual with a heroic redemption. Or consider the journey of Oprah Winfrey. She overcame poverty, physical abuse, neglect, and sexual abuse to become an actor, talk-show host, philanthropist, and media executive.

This concept of redemption is a Jungian archetype. It represents a universal theme. People aspire to overcome obstacles and find progress. The famous psychologist Carl Rogers declared that people are basically good and strive toward self-actualization.[2] So, in an effort to grow and heal, the belief that people can change is key to interpersonal forgiveness. Forgiveness can be a hero's journey, both for the victim and the perpetrator. Each person can overcome adversity, grow, and change. Often, our capacity to forgive can seem heroic. Consider the actions of the congregants at the Al Salam Mosque in Fort Smith, AR (described in Chapter 2), who help the offender in his redemptive journey. The offender expressed remorse, sought forgiveness, and made a change. Both the victims of the crime who offer the perpetrator a path toward redemption and the offender make a heroic journey.

In these examples, we see people who at one time committed harm toward another choose a redemptive path and hopefully become a better person. Most important, this redemptive path of the offender was recognized by the person or people harmed, and they acknowledged this change. In offering forgiveness, the victims are viewed as making a heroic journey as well. Forgiveness goes beyond understanding the perpetrator. The offering of forgiveness and reconciliation requires strength not only to recover from a past offense but also to provide the offender a chance to make things right at the risk of further harm.

Redemption may not always be an interpersonal journey, however. In the previous examples, both the offender and the victim seem to be open to a similar path. The victim has indicated that there is some benefit to reconciliation. If reconciliation is going to be beneficial, this will usually involve evidence of some remorse or change in behavior on the part of the offender. When an offender is remorseful and commits to a change in behavior, reconciliation becomes a possibility. At some point, there will be a *heroic confrontation*.

Perhaps this idea seems a little far-fetched. As a clinician, I see my clients as heroes. The willingness to address problems head-on and commit to making a change is a heroic journey. If it were easy, the client would have already accomplished whatever change was desired. When overcome with frustration and an inability to change, a client often decides to seek help and be vulnerable. If you are reading this and thinking about how you were harmed, who hurt you, and what your feelings are regarding that person who harmed you, then take time to consider how far you have come and grown in the process. In fact, why not think of yourself as a hero, or at the very least, as being on a heroic journey!

As depicted in the FRM, there is a meeting with the perpetrator—a moment where one who has been harmed and believes that reconciliation may be beneficial must recognize whether the perpetrator has demonstrated remorse and change. We will discuss how this is evaluated later in the chapter, but for now, just consider the action of confronting an offender.

Confronting any fear can be daunting, and this is especially true when the fear being confronted is a person who caused pain or harm. Often, a person who was harmful (whether physically, emotionally, financially, or otherwise) exerted some type of power. Not only is confrontation daunting on an emotional level, but also the fear of further harm is an enormous obstacle to try to overcome. However, the hope of reconciliation lies within this confrontation.

While the FRM depicts this as a single stage, keep in mind that the meeting with the perpetrator is just as much of a process as anything else. To think of this as a single meeting would be naive. Taking time to discern the extent of remorse and how or if the offender has changed is paramount. This is an important undertaking that should not be rushed. The reward of a reconciled relationship, perhaps one that is even stronger, is exciting, but relationships cannot always be reconciled, even if the benefits are obvious.

Let's reflect on Derek for a moment. Recall that Derek had a history of drug use, dealing, and physical altercations at home. He was particularly angry with his mother, but he took ownership that he also overreacted. Initially, he focused only on his frustration that she would interfere with his plans, claiming, "She's always in my business." But given Derek's history, his mother intervening appeared reasonable. It turns out, however, that Derek's anger toward his mother was not completely unfounded. Derek's mother was quick to provide discipline and structure, but she was not one to show affection.

Derek continued in counseling. He identified that his mother was quick to anger and criticize but rarely, if ever, expressed praise or showed affection. Derek figured his mother was depressed, and she would not do anything about it.

One particular aspect of Derek's therapy centered around his care for his mother after she was diagnosed with bone cancer. Derek's mother was in considerable pain and confined to her bed, where she was getting hospice in her home. Derek would sit with her every day. He even indicated to this counselor that he felt like he was finally connecting with her. "She appreciates me coming over and being with her. We are finally acting like a mother and son. I've gotten more support from her as she is dying than I ever got when she was living."

During one of Derek's last visits with his mother, he sat next to her and told her, "I love you, Mom." She said nothing in return, though he was certain he heard her. His mother died about 2 weeks later. "She never said it back to me," he said to his counselor while staring at the floor. "She could not say she loved me. She was a bitch 'til the bitter end."

In our earlier conceptualization of Derek, he seems antisocial, uninsightful, and abusive. But perhaps now we can empathize with Derek a bit more. Moreover, we see Derek made a sincere attempt to reconnect with his mother, but his mother ultimately refuses and continues to withhold the affection that Derek craves. Despite his growth and change, he is unable to control the change within his mother.

So, what is Derek's heroic journey? He certainly made positive changes in his life. He saw reconciliation as a beneficial process. He made a heroic confrontation, attempting to reconnect with his mother. Despite Derek's modeling of remorse and change in his journey, Derek's mother was not able to show a reciprocal process. Still, Derek has come a long way, but his heroic journey will likely be more intrapersonal, rather than interpersonal.

What Happens When Reconciliation Is Not Beneficial?

Reconciliation may not be the appropriate, healthy outcome. If a relationship was unhappy with negative feelings about the offender, or there is no remorse or change from the offender, then reconciliation is likely a poor option. Let's look at Deanna's situation again. She experienced a breakup, was repeatedly abused by her ex-boyfriend, and suffered from addiction, which was initiated during her relationship with her ex-boyfriend. Moreover, Deanna's ex-boyfriend is unapologetic. Sometimes, the offender may still be a jerk. Deanna's ex is actively using drugs and shows no remorse or intent to change his behavior. This is clearly an unhealthy relationship for Deanna, and if Deanna were to pursue reconciliation and an interpersonal path with respect to forgiveness, she would likely be putting herself in further harm.

So, what happens when reconciliation is beneficial, but the offender does not demonstrate any change or remorse? Whereas in the case of Deanna, reconciliation was not beneficial and would be deemed extremely unhealthy, sometimes the person who was hurt or harmed can still envision a situation in which reconciliation would be beneficial.

For example, with Sheila's situation, we have spent a lot of time examining forgiveness as it relates to Sheila and her father, especially with the pressure Sheila received from her mother. But let's ask a different question: Should Sheila forgive her mother?

Sheila would like to have the love and support of her mother. Sheila's mother may not have believed that her husband abused his daughter, or she may have believed Sheila but placed her own need—that of keeping the family intact—above the needs of her daughter. Either way, regardless of Sheila wanting the support of her mother and seeing a reconciled relationship as beneficial, Sheila's mother does not change course. She does not express remorse or change her behavior. When Sheila leaves the hospital, she does not go to live with her mother but lives with extended family instead.

Part of this third phase in the FRM, therefore, takes into consideration that regardless of whether a victim perceives reconciliation as beneficial or nonbeneficial, the outcome could be the same. *If reconciliation is perceived as beneficial and the offender does not change and show remorse, or if reconciliation is simply not beneficial, a person who has experienced hurt or harm is in the same place—needing to address that what was expected or wanted from the offender is not going to be given.* This is a potential outcome with all types of issues with respect to conflict and forgiveness.

Even less severe issues, such as conflict at work or being cut off while driving, often inspire some type of recognition from the offender, only to be left with the fact that no sense of remorse or apology is forthcoming. Perhaps you or someone you know has little tolerance for poor driving. This individual is driving appropriately on a main road and suddenly gets cut off by an unobservant driver. Were it not for the skills and attentiveness of the careful driver, there would have been a collision. But there was not. Nevertheless, the careful driver is now mad and honking at the errant driver. To the careful driver's dismay, there is no recognition that the errant driver nearly caused a collision. So, the careful driver quickly switches lanes, slams on the accelerator, hits the horn, and through the window flips the errant driver off and mouths "f*** you!" The errant driver responds by returning a similar gesture.

So, mission accomplished?

Clearly not much that transpired in this scenario is positive. No one has changed their belief system. As a matter of fact, the action that ensued may have been even more dangerous than the initial issue of simply being inattentive. Moreover, whatever the careful driver wanted from the errant driver was not met, and the situation escalated without much of a satisfactory resolution. There was no remorse or change from the offender. The errant driver is not likely to become more careful. And yet, both people will likely drive again and engage in similar behaviors in the future. Not only is the errant driver not likely to change, but what about the supposedly careful driver? Is that person likely to change? Coming to terms with the idea that what is wanted or needed is not likely to occur is key to addressing a lack of remorse and change from the offender.

PROCESSING UNPAID DEBT

Let's re-emphasize an important point: *If reconciliation is perceived as beneficial and the offender does not change and show remorse, or if reconciliation is simply not beneficial, a person who has experienced hurt or harm is in the same place—needing to address that what was expected or wanted from the offender is not going to be given.* This is the realization that what was wanted from someone else simply is not going to happen, and this recognition can come across in many forms, such as anger, fear, grief, or even relief. In the FRM, what one is expecting and not receiving is referred to as the *debt*. There are many examples of unpaid debt, particularly when referring to money or something tangible. But unpaid debt can be emotional as well, such as not receiving support, love, safety, or care.

The realization that what was wanted from someone will never be given can be a poignant, sad moment. Consider a time you have experienced pain or even trauma from someone. You want an apology or perhaps something even more from this person. Seeing reconciliation as beneficial but receiving nothing of the sort from the offender can feel like a gut-punch, and may even result in feelings of revictimization, such as in circumstances in which someone is withholding from you love, affection, or validation .

Furthermore, the inability or unwillingness for an offender to express remorse and change behavior is not within the power of the victim and often results in the victim experiencing feelings of guilt, self-blame, and the tendency to turn inward. Addressing feelings of inadequacy, self-blame, and guilt is important, with the goal of countering such feelings with a recognition of the fallibility of the offender.

At other times, a victim may recognize, sometimes quite easily, that reconciliation is not beneficial. Moving forward with the recognition that what was wanted from the offender will never be received can be empowering, particularly when the offender wishes to pursue reconciliation, but the victim chooses an intrapersonal path. A victim can make a choice to forgo the relationship with the offender and therefore be free of the burden of the relationship and the expectations. We can look at situations of abuse, such as with Deanna, as an example. The offender—in this case her ex-boyfriend—might pursue reconciliation with Deanna. However, Deanna recognizes the unhealthy dynamics of the relationship and the previous empty promises of her ex-boyfriend to make changes.

She therefore decides to recognize that he is unable or unwilling to change and assumes the power in the relationship by moving forward without him. But this is not simply a matter of leaving the relationship hurt or angry. Intrapersonal forgiveness includes the release of anger or hurt. It is the ability to move forward with a healthy disposition. This process begins by processing unpaid debt.

Processing unpaid debt may be best conceptualized as working through grief,[3] and grief can include an array of emotions, such as anger and depression.[4] As mentioned earlier in the book and similar to all other parts of the FRM, grieving is a process and requires work, time, and patience. Grief can be extremely complex, and certainly issues of conflict and forgiveness can be quite different from issues of grief and loss, but the idea of working through stages that address the loss of a relationship or the realization that one will not receive what was once hoped for is relevant for processing unpaid debt. Kübler-Ross's initial model was published in 1969 and has survived the test of time and remains firmly grounded in theory of working through grief and loss. Kübler-Ross's model was briefly mentioned in Chapter 2 with respect to working through anger. The five phases, including denial, anger, bargaining, depression, and acceptance, may apply here as well. Deanna's case study could provide an example of these phases.

Deanna does not simply accept that what was wanted, earned, or deserved will never come to pass from her ex-boyfriend. Despite going through a breakup, she continues to live with him. She demonstrates some denial, believing that her ex can or will change or that the relationship is not over. She exhibits anger toward him because of an inability or unwillingness to change, and his empty promises to change and failure to do so might need to be processed and worked through. She even makes a last-ditch effort to convince him to change and succumbs to feelings of depression and low self-worth at her inability to convince him and heal the relationship. Eventually, she moves to acceptance, recognizing that what she wanted from the relationship she will never get, and she can begin her own journey toward health and a better sense of self-worth.

RECOGNIZING REMORSE AND CHANGE FROM THE OFFENDER

When reconciliation is not beneficial, processing unpaid debt is the logical next step. Particularly in situations of repeated abuse or trauma, reconciliation with the perpetrator is not a healthy option or viable alternative. We see this in Sheila's and Deanna's cases, where they were both abused and the offenders were neither remorseful nor demonstrating any intentions of change.

However, when determining remorse and change from an offender is pertinent to choosing an interpersonal or intrapersonal path toward forgiveness, taking time to evaluate thoughts and beliefs about an offender is essential to the process. Although you can never be certain what someone thinks or believes, you can observe the person's behavior.

Contrition. If reconciliation is going to be successful, there should be some recognition from the offender about wrongdoing. We have all had experiences of empty apologies, and the expectation that the offender goes beyond an apology is appropriate. Apologies can be empty—"I am sorry, but . . ." is not a real apology but rather an effort to justify one's behavior. One way to evaluate the extent to which an expression of remorse is sincere is to look for congruence between feelings and behavior. When someone is demonstrating sincerity with an apology, consider whether the apology can be heard, seen, and felt. What was observed when the apology was made? Were the offender's actions consistent with the words spoken? Was an apology made with an expression of sadness for the offense, or was the apology made with a smirk or sense of convenience? Some apologies may feel forced because the person making the apology is hoping for something in return—a gesture of gratitude or a reciprocal behavior. True remorse is an expression made without expectation of getting something in return. The expression of remorse should be felt by both the offender and the victim.

Humility. Remorse and arrogance are not a good mix. Remorse and change do not come easily. So, there should be acknowledgment that there is work to do, perhaps individually or relationally. For example, Jerome and Maria both experienced infidelity in their marriage. Certainly, they could benefit from working together as a couple, but they might also have to do their own work individually, especially if anger persists. Sometimes, hurt and anger are obstacles to the desire to reconcile.

Recognition of the difficulty toward change is not a sign of weakness but rather a signal that the individual is realistic and aware of the work ahead. For instance, individuals who have struggled with addiction might feel very confident in their ability to maintain sobriety and verbalize a plan to stay clean and sober. Unfortunately, this overconfidence often results in placing themselves in untenable situations where relapse becomes more likely. Individuals who are cautious and even a bit anxious about their ability to stay clean and sober will be more likely to take the necessary steps to stay clean and sober.

In this regard, humility coupled with a moderate level of anxiety can be a positive attribute to creating change. When anxiety is low, people put in less effort to change; change is less likely to occur because individuals likely feel less pressure to change. As anxiety increases to a moderate level, the likelihood of change is at the highest level. Some anxiety can have a positive influence, such as when you want to impress someone and you place your best foot forward to be seen in a positive light. But as anxiety increases even more, it can become debilitating, thereby once again making change harder and less likely. When we sense a moderate level of anxiety, along with a degree of humility, that can be a good indication of sincerity about remorse and change.

Change. There are many factors that lead to change: external pressures, new insights, traumatic experiences, mortality, hitting rock bottom, and so forth. Common to each of these issues is discomfort—discomfort with an environment, a situation, a person, a personal behavior, or something else.[5] People are motivated to change because of discomfort. From the simplest things like rolling over during sleep to making job changes or life changes, such transitions occur because of discomfort or the ability to become even more comfortable, which could be due to the desire to change personally, interpersonally, financially, spiritually, or otherwise. When addressing issues of conflict or forgiveness, change will occur, whether it is interpersonal or intrapersonal change. With interpersonal change, the dynamics of the relationship can evolve because of a healthier mindset from the victim, such as setting firmer interpersonal boundaries, or from the offender, who desires to repair the relationship and recognizes the need for personal growth. Often, people become complicit with unhealthy or dysfunctional relationships because it is what they are used to—their sense of homeostasis (or balance) is based on the dysfunction of the relationship. And when that dysfunction is interrupted, the relationship often can feel worse before it gets better.

Recall that Sheila was hospitalized because of threats of suicide after her father was removed from the home and she was not receiving emotional support from her mother. In the early moments of her therapy, she was dreading family sessions with her mother and testifying in court, as well as the upheaval in her family and the uncertainty of what was going to happen next. All of this stress, on top of the abuse she experienced, made her situation feel even worse. In the experience of trauma, initiating change may lead to more discomfort initially, not less, and having a support system in place is essential. I told Sheila that I understand her situation feels worse right now, but it will get better. That honesty and affirmation seemed to help. When addressing trauma and confronting a perpetrator, do so with the intention of making improvements, but understand that discomfort may increase in the short-term.

Honesty. Back in Chapter 1, I introduced the story of testifying in court on Sheila's case. Her father denied Sheila's allegations, and in court, the father's attorney asked me why I believe Sheila, and I pointed to three factors that influence my belief in the trustworthiness of my client: consistency, feasibility, and congruence. In short, Sheila's disclosure remained very consistent in light of numerous interviews with Child Protective Services workers, legal personnel, and medical/psychiatric personnel. Sheila's allegations were not unlike other allegations that occur. Finally, Sheila's affect—the emotions she displayed—were consistent with what might be expected when recalling a traumatic situation, either distressed or detached.

But when confronting a perpetrator and evaluating the sincerity of change, the offender might very well be demonstrating these traits. Detecting honesty is not easy, and perpetrators, especially those who have engaged in offending behaviors over a longer period of time, are likely polished in their presentation of demonstrating sincerity. How often does a victim hear from an offender consistent sincerity about plans to do better, change behavior, and express remorse for past behaviors, only to have the perpetrator fall short and re-engage in the same offenses?

Why a person fails to change despite promises might be due to intentional manipulation, but it can also be due to unintended personal failings. Derek, for example, did not get sober after his first treatment. He had relapses, and change was difficult. This pattern of relapse was processed with his counselor.

COUNSELOR: What happened that led to this most recent relapse?

DEREK: This is such crap and b.s. Nothing happened. I told you what you wanted to hear. You believed me. And I went out and did what I wanted!

COUNSELOR: I guess that is one way to look at it.

DEREK: What do you mean?

COUNSELOR: Well, I heard you in sessions. I truly believe you wanted to change. And when you tried, you found out it was hard. And you relapsed. But it is a lot easier for you to blame me for your failure than it is for you to take responsibility for it and admit you failed.

DEREK: Damn!

Derek's modus operandi was to externalize—to blame others rather than accept responsibility for himself. And this is not so uncommon in abusive relationships. Does the offender not change because of the intention of being manipulative, or does the offender not change because of personal failing? Although the latter option could engender more sympathy or understanding from the victim, the answer may not be that important because the outcome is the same—a reoffense toward the victim.

Furthermore, the experience of childhood trauma, desire for intimacy, fear of loneliness, belief that violence in relationships was normal, low self-esteem, and absence of viable alternatives are common characteristics among individuals who experience revictimization.[6,7] Even without the promise to change, the courage to remove oneself from an unhealthy relationship should not be underestimated.

Nonexploitative behavior. One of the reasons issues of conflict and forgiveness are difficult is the sense of betrayal and of being used. A recognized concept in both therapy, healing, and healthy relationships is *mutuality*—the idea that we do not look only at how others affect us but also at how we affect others.[8,9] Mutuality is an important component in healthy, nonexploitative relationships. Often, when relationships are exploitative, it is because of the one-sidedness of the relationship. Specifically, the offender has more impact on the victim, and the victim has a lack of impact on the offender. When mutuality is present, the impact and connection between two people are reciprocal.[10]

When attempting to reconcile a relationship in which there was a power differential, or a lack of mutuality, reflecting on how the power dynamics will play out differently in the future is an important consideration. Even less severe situations, such as when we feel upset from a lack of acknowledgment in our work or interpersonal relationships, or when someone borrowed from you and never returned what was borrowed, can be exploitative. The expression of gratitude can sometimes go a long way in preventing feelings of exploitation or repairing a breached relationship. Relationships are key to feelings of connection and promoting growth and change.[11] With that being said, when we experience feelings of exploitation, our connection with others may be breached, and our relationships with others may be less likely to be mended or reconciled.

Moral behavior. Sometimes, the expectation that a person apologize, express remorse, and make a change is based on a moral foundation. In relationships, we expect people to do the right thing, and when they do not, we might feel disheartened. Although an offense that harms a relationship can be a single occurrence, the nature of such offenses often transcends to others areas. The unhealthy relationship between a perpetrator and offender often extends to other areas, such as work relationships, interactions with friends, and relationships with children or other family members. Hence, when considering whether to reconcile a relationship, examining the extent to which an offender is rectifying relationships and changing behaviors in a more global context can be helpful to evaluating the sincerity of the offender about remorse and change.

Even though Derek's attempt to reconcile with his mother became a more intrapersonal journey, because of his mother's inability or unwillingness to change her behavior, Derek did demonstrate changes in other areas. He quit using drugs and alcohol, and he made personal improvements, working toward his education and establishing himself in a career. Derek's changes were not singular in focus, but he demonstrated a moral understanding of his transgressions and worked to make amends, which had a larger effect on his own well-being and relationships with others.

UNDERSTANDING YOUR JOURNEY

Whether in our interpersonal relationships, work relationships, or hobbies and service activities, everything we do is relational in some way. Even with very personal experiences, such as mindfulness, meditation, or yoga, you likely learned these activities from a mentor or even in a class. These personal activities are learned through relationships! With all of the relationships we experience, conflict is inevitable. Moreover, the sources of the conflict—people who appear to direct the discomfort, pain, or harm in one's life—may not see themselves as wrong, and even if they do, they may not change. Even if reconciliation appears to be beneficial from the perspective of the one who was hurt, reconciliation cannot occur in a vacuum. The offender gets to make a choice, and the individual who was hurt may feel somewhat powerless about the offender's choice. But even if power appears lessened at an interpersonal level, there is always power at the intrapersonal level.

You have the power to not accept reconciliation without remorse and change. Essentially, you have some power to hold the offender to a degree of accountability. However, this requires follow-through on the part of the offender. Remember the *principle of least interest* from Chapter 5? If the desire to reconcile the relationship is stronger than the need to experience remorse and change from the perpetrator, the victim cedes power in the relationship. Such a decision could be a predisposing factor to revictimization.

You have the power to choose the path. At the beginning of this chapter, two alternate paths were introduced. One path is based on the perceived benefit of reconciliation but requires a confrontation with the offender and an evaluation of the extent the offender will change—a decision made by the offender. The alternative path might be something the victim chooses or perhaps is forced into as a result of holding one's ground. On one hand, reconciliation may not be perceived as beneficial. On the other hand, reconciliation may be perceived as beneficial as long as the offender commits and demonstrates remorse and change. Without the offender's commitment and demonstration of remorse and change and the desire of the victim to hold firm to this request, the remaining alternative is an intrapersonal path.

We began this chapter identifying that the third phase of the FRM is different from the previous phases. The third phase may include an external process—one that is not under your control. When choosing reconciliation of a relationship, the perpetrator may or may not choose to express remorse and change of behavior, which may be a determinant for how a victim may proceed through the FRM. Regardless of feelings related to reconciliation, the power to choose reconciliation is shared between the victim and the perpetrator. You may decide that reconciliation is not beneficial, which releases you to an intrapersonal process of forgiveness by processing unpaid debt. Or you may decide reconciliation is beneficial, but end up in the same place—an intrapersonal process—because the offender will not change. Of course, there is the possibility that by opening the door to reconciliation, a relationship can be rebuilt.

You may need to come to terms with the idea that what you wanted from this person you will never receive. Or you may need to work on forging a new path with a person who caused hurt or pain. These processes will be covered in Chapter 7.

NOTES

1. Jung, C. G., & Franz, M. V. (1968). *Man and his symbols*. New York: Dell.
2. Rogers, C. R. (1961). *On becoming a person*. Houghton Mifflin.
3. Balkin et al., 2009.
4. Kübler-Ross, 2005.
5. Kottler & Balkin, 2020.
6. Edwards, K. M., Gidycz, C. A., & Murphy, M. J. (2011). College women's stay/ leave decisions in abusive dating relationships: A prospective analysis of an expanded investment model. *Journal of Interpersonal Violence, 26*(7), 1446– 1462. https://doi-org.umiss.idm.oclc.org/10.1177/0886260510369131
7. Valdez, C. E., Ban Hong (Phylice) Lim, & Lilly, M. M. (2013). "It's going to make the whole tower crooked": Victimization trajectories in IPV. *Journal*

of *Family Violence*, 28(2), 131–140. https://doi-org.umiss.idm.oclc.org/10.1007/s10896-012-9476-7

8. Duffey, T., & Somody, C. (2011). The role of relational-cultural theory in mental health counseling. *Journal of Mental Health Counseling, 33*(3), 223–242. https://doi-org.umiss.idm.oclc.org/10.17744/mehc.33.3.c10410226u275647

9. Jordan, 1991.

10. Duffey & Somody, 2011.

11. Kottler & Balkin, 2017.

Chapter 7

Choosing the Outcome

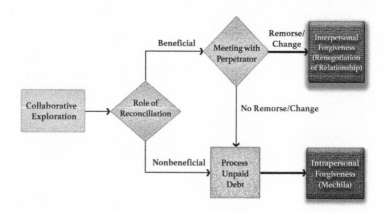

In the final stage of the Forgiveness Reconciliation Model (FRM), we return to an internal process. The previous, third phase of the FRM was different from the first and second phases because the remorse and change of the offender are outside the control of those who have been harmed. Working through issues of conflict and forgiveness was described as an external process in the third phase. The fourth phase of the FRM—*choosing the outcome*—is one that is within our control. Approaching the final phase can be both empowering and heartbreaking. Empowerment may come from the ability to work toward reconstituting a relationship or from letting go of enmity toward a person who has caused harm or pain.

Regardless of whether one decides to renegotiate a relationship through reconciliation or to work through an intrapersonal process of forgiveness, forgiveness provides an opportunity strengthen one's emotional fortitude, which derives from overcoming an offense and relinquishing ill will toward another. In addition, it is the person who has been harmed who has the final say about how to move forward in the forgiveness process.

The fourth phase of the FRM presents a dichotomized choice: Either an interpersonal or an intrapersonal path of forgiveness will be forged. Whether a person who has experienced pain or harm from someone else is renegotiating a relationship or addressing unresolved grief, the relationship with the perpetrator is going to be different.

INTERPERSONAL FORGIVENESS: THE RENEGOTIATED RELATIONSHIP

Throughout the explanation of the FRM, the *process* of forgiveness has been emphasized, and the focus on process in this final stage remains pertinent. For example, when recognizing the benefits of reconciliation and the remorse and change in the offender, an individual is not likely to suddenly declare, "We've reached a new point in our relationship, and everything is good!" Rather, the renegotiation of the relationship is an action in which a victim decides to reinvest in the relationship. More colloquially, the jury is still out as to whether this is going to work or not. When making a decision to renegotiate a relationship, there is no promise of success or that one cannot go back to the previous stage of evaluating remorse and change of the offender and come to a different decision all together.

Let's re-examine the experiences of Alexander Davis, who vandalized the Al Salam Mosque, wrote a letter of apology, and received both advocacy and assistance in moving forward from the members at Al Salam Mosque. The US Federal Bureau of Investigation (FBI) has defined a *hate crime* as "a traditional offense like murder, arson, or vandalism with an added element of bias." While the vandalism of the Al Salam Mosque (described in Chapter 2) was never identified as a hate crime by the FBI, the event fits the definition. Individuals who engage in these crimes attempt to instill fear on their victims. Members of the Al Salam Mosque likely felt a combination of fear, anger, and sadness on hearing and seeing this egregious act, as well as a sense of relief and hope for justice when the vandals were arrested. If this experience ended at this point, where there was no expression of remorse from Davis and reciprocal acts by members of the Al Salam Mosque, then there is no story. But, there is a story.

Members of Al Salam Mosque recently had heard a sermon about forgiveness when Davis wrote a heartfelt apology about the vandalism, and from that point, a series of events led to interpersonal forgiveness and a renegotiation of the relationship. This relationship was not going back to what it was but rather would be transformed into reciprocal actions of sincere care and gratitude. The relationship between the members of Al Salam Mosque and Alexander Davis changed, and the individuals invested in this relationship grew. The growth of the respective individuals came from each side making a heroic journey, as referenced in Chapter 6. Not only did the victims of the offense journey forward in their expression of care and willingness to forgive, but also the perpetrator of this offense initiated a healing process.

Perhaps the same can be said for Jerome and Maria, who each experienced infidelity in their marriage but made the decision to renegotiate their relationship and try to save their marriage. When there is a breach in a relationship, couples may strive to "go back to the way things used to be." But such a development is unlikely. Furthermore, just because a relationship is breached does not mean it is forever broken. Couples like Jerome and Maria can heal their relationship and become stronger as a couple, but resetting the relationship to how the couple functioned in the past is not likely, and couples should be prepared for this.

INTRAPERSONAL FORGIVENESS: A RE-EXAMINATION OF MECHILA, THE FORGIVENESS OF DEBT

Mechila is a Hebrew word introduced in Chapters 2 and 3 and translates to "forgiveness of debt."[1] With mechila, there is no mandate that a relationship should be reconciled; rather, what is owed to the victim is forgiven. In other words, the victim no longer expects anything from the perpetrator and relinquishes both debt and feelings of ill will toward the offender. Not only is the perpetrator relieved of a debt to the victim, but the victim is taking steps to also relieve any emotional burden being carried toward the offender. The forgiveness of debt, therefore, can be made for a few reasons.

Retributive and Restorative Justice

Recall from Chapter 5 that retributive justice is concerned with the extent to which punishment is fair, and restorative justice focuses on the rehabilitation of the offender. In retributive justice, not every act requiring justice or fairness should be framed as punishment. For example, I borrowed your lawn mower; I broke your lawn mower;

I repaired your lawnmower. We're good, right? I made restitution, but I may not have done this under duress, coercion, or fear of punishment. In this case, no harm was made, and the situation was easy to restore. I have likely shown myself to be trustworthy. Breaking your lawnmower might have been an inconvenience, but the situation has been remedied. In this case, our relationship is likely to continue and may even get better.

Restorative justice applies to the events with Alexander Davis and his expression of remorse toward members of Al Salam Mosque. However, if the notion of restorative justice were applied to the marital issues of Jerome and Maria, a more complex issue would be at hand. Jerome and Maria each experienced problems in their relationship, and trust between them was eroded. Whereas the members of Al Salam Mosque and Davis had no relationship before the vandalism, Jerome and Maria were in a committed relationship before their infidelity. So, the dynamics are indeed different. In this case, an individual who was harmed by another is looking for evidence that trust can be rebuilt. How that happens likely is as unique as the circumstances that can cause a breach in a relationship. This is a good moment to be reminded that being a forgiving or trusting person is not the goal. Issues of conflict and forgiveness are context-driven and unique processes.

Retributive or Restorative Justice Is Not Possible

Both retributive and restorative justice require an interpersonal process in which the perpetrator and victim renegotiate their relationship. The reality is that not every conflict can be resolved through interpersonal forms of justice. But as shown throughout this book, sometimes an intrapersonal model to address conflict and forgiveness is more appropriate.

As retributive justice is framed around fairness, there are numerous ways fairness can be appropriated. For example, fairness could be appropriated through punishment, as with Dylann Roof being sentenced to death for the murders of members of the Emanuel African Methodist Episcopal Church. Of course, retributive justice can be relegated to far less severe circumstances, such as restitution for an offense or even mistake that must be addressed. We see this in the previous example with the broken lawnmower. Some offenses can be rectified.

Naturally, there are times when restitution should be made but cannot be afforded. For example, a friend borrows your car but is in a car accident, and the car is totaled. Maybe insurance covers it, but maybe you are still at a loss, and your friend does not have the money to repay it. You could be out thousands of dollars! You have to decide whether your relationship is irreparably harmed over money. Unfortunately, these types of issues occur across many different scenarios within business, families, friends, or other ventures. Common to them all is that a debt that is owed cannot be repaid by the offender.

Sometimes, the inability to make restitution is not possible because what was taken or the nature of the offense can never be repaid. Previously, we explored issues of trauma, abuse, and infidelity with respect to offenses in which a notion of justice is elusive, but other forms of offenses, such as neglect, slander, or insensitivity toward someone, also fit into this scenario. In the FRM, an intrapersonal path should be pursued in the following circumstances:

- Trust cannot be re-established because of repeated offenses.
- The offender is unwilling or unable to communicate or demonstrate remorse and change.
- The victim chooses not to re-establish a relationship with the perpetrator.

Reinforcements and Challenges to Interpersonal Forgiveness and Mechila

Certainly, there are challenges to pursuing interpersonal forgiveness. The tasks of rebuilding trust, overcoming emotional barriers, and renegotiating a relationship with a person who has been harmful are difficult. Yet, very often the outward appearance of re-establishing a relationship can be reinforcing because a person who is reconciling a relationship might feel unsolicited support from others. For example, the outcome of Alexander Davis's relationship with members of Al Salam Mosque is a feel-good story, and perhaps the type of narrative that other people support and discuss enthusiastically. In a similar vein, admiration for an individual who fights for healing and reconciliation in a relationship, such as a partnership or marriage, might receive positive support from friends, family, or the community.

On the other hand, mechila—the forgiveness of debt and pursuit of an intrapersonal path—may get a bad rap. Admiration is often expressed toward people who recover from trauma. Their strengths are recognized, and their journey may be used as examples for others. Quite often, however, when people leave a relationship, they may feel broken. We can look at Sheila and see that even though she came forward about the abuse by her father, she was in fact having a lot of difficulty. She was suicidal and surrounded by conflict. Sheila expressed that when coming forward about the abuse, her situation felt worse, not better, especially given the lack of support from her mother. Deanna is another example: She wanted to leave a relationship but remained living with her ex-boyfriend. Her situation worsened, as did the abuse.

Let's be clear. By coming forward, Sheila is demonstrating strength and fortitude. And given the circumstances she is facing, who can really blame her for feeling hopeless? But as much as we might acknowledge Sheila's strength, those in her immediate system are not reinforcing her decisions. She doesn't feel strong. Quite the opposite, actually: She feels worthless at times.

Leaving or ending a relationship requires considerable strength and fortitude that often go unrecognized by the people closest to us. The result is that mechila may seem less than an honorable journey. Such a decision to end a relationship may go against familial, social, religious, or cultural norms. Unhealthy messages might be reinforced:

- You're giving up.
- You're a quitter.
- You don't walk away from _____ (e.g., friends, family, spouse, partner).
- Think about the people you are hurting.
- How can you do this to someone?
- By leaving, you will harm _____ (e.g., kids, family, friends).

The recognition that a relationship is unhealthy may be complicated by additional unhealthy systems. For example, individuals in abusive relationships often experienced an abusive family system. Individuals who find themselves in unhealthy situations should be cautious about the messages they hear that reinforce unhealthy decisions. Separating oneself from unhealthy relationships, not just the relationship that is causing the most harm but also the secondary relationships that reinforce unhealthy decisions, can be difficult. An array of problems, such as addiction, trauma, neglect, abuse, depression, and stress, may be related to systemic issues. Family, work, and interpersonal relationships may be antecedents to these problems.

The heroic journey referred to in Chapter 6 needs to have a starting point, but the onset of this journey, particularly when the journey is more intrapersonal, may be far more stressful in the beginning when the support systems in place enable the dysfunctional relationship with the offender.[1]

Of course, interpersonal forgiveness is not always viewed positively, and intrapersonal forgiveness is not always viewed negatively. Continuing to stay in a relationship with an abusive partner or spouse certainly is unhealthy. Pursuing an intrapersonal path would seem be a healthier decision. Once again, the support system can play a role, especially when the support system is positive and can provide reassurance and encouragement for healthier decisions.

Pursuing interpersonal forgiveness may not be all it's cracked up to be. Relationships can be difficult to renegotiate. An offender may demonstrate some change and remorse, but is it enough? What was envisioned for the relationship may not reflect what actually transpires. Sometimes, the renegotiation of a relationship results in accepting the relationship as it is—in other words, this is as good as it is going to get. Such a scenario might require a combined approach to interpersonal forgiveness and mechila. The victim from an offense works with the offender to renegotiate the relationship but also recognizes that there is compromise in this process. Trust may be built, but the extent of change being sought is not demonstrated. As the individual who was harmed seeks healing as well as growth in the relationship, there is also a realization that relationships are imperfect and fallible. Accepting the person as is and without ill will is necessary and even relationship-enhancing.

An intrapersonal process of forgiveness may seem difficult. When interpersonal forgiveness is pursued, there is a relational process involved. Two people are in it together, which may have a positive or negative outcome. But with mechila, the person who was harmed chooses to move forward alone and must address the unresolved grief of not getting what was wanted from the relationship, and particularly from the offender. Hence, mechila can feel lonely, especially when the focus is on a bad choice or a failed relationship. Let's take a look at what needs to happen for mechila to be empowering and durable.

Relinquishing debt. Let's just be clear here: It really sucks when someone owes you something, and you know you are never going to get it, whether it is money, a favor, some obligation, an apology, emotional support, or something else. This step requires a cognitive realization and an emotional acceptance. You might be angry, hurt, fearful, or traumatized that someone wronged you or caused you harm. And that pain or hurt often influences your decisions and actions. But the behaviors you engage in should probably not come from a place of hurt or anger. Rather, consider how future behaviors you engage in will affect the situation. Will they help or hurt? Perhaps what is needed is to come to terms with the pain you are experiencing and accept it because changing someone and their behaviors toward you is quite difficult.

Sometimes, this realization occurs because of the recognition that what was done cannot possibly be rectified. This is certainly true in cases of harm or trauma. Other times, some type of restitution could be made, but it is just not going to happen. What if all that is wanted is a simple apology, but that apology is not going to come? Or, it could be a financial debt that could be repaid, but the person will not or cannot repay it.

Sheila wanted support from her mother after disclosing the abuse by her father. At some point, Sheila had to come to terms with the idea that her mother was not going to be emotionally supportive. Jerome and Maria each had to recognize that their ideal of marriage was not happening in their marriage, and while the marriage could be repaired, the infidelity that took place could not be undone. Derek recognized that the reconciliation he desired with his mother would not occur, and although this hurt deeply, he could not control her behavior and responses to his overtures.

Regardless of the situation, there is a recognition from the victim that what was desired, or perhaps even might still be desired at the present, is not going to happen. So, why hold onto the debt? Consider that expecting someone to pay a debt—to provide what is owed—may not be as empowering as originally contrived. Perhaps you have had the experience of someone or something holding a debt over your head. When it is an organization, like a hefty bill to be paid, that organization may hold certain power—such as damaging your credit or taking you to court. So, you comply with the demands. But sometimes, there is no power in collecting a debt. What is owed to you is simply not going to be given, and there is not a damn thing you can do about it! In situations such as this, who truly has the power? Despite whether you feel something legitimately is owed to you, it is the offender who holds the power—the power to repay the debt.

Moreover, there can be a revictimization effect by expecting some type of repayment or restitution and not getting it. Not only is the debt to be repaid being withheld, but also the offender is taking license to reoffend. Hence, a bad situation becomes even more detrimental and unhealthy. So, relinquishing debt is a means to gain control over the situation. By recognizing that you are not likely to get what you feel is deserved, you become empowered to say, "I no longer expect anything from you." This recognition is not devoid of feeling, such as anger, sadness, or other emotion. Rather, this is a grieving process.

Resolving grief. After the cognitive realization of relinquishing debt is made, there is still the emotional baggage that remains. Even after realizing that a debt will never be repaid and assuming power to relinquish that debt, one is still left with a sense of loss that can manifest itself through anger, sadness, despair, frustration, or any other emotion. Perhaps the best way to conceptualize working through this emotional minefield is through the lens of grief. Throughout this book, the issue of grief is mentioned in the various stages of the FRM. This might include working through various emotions associated with grief, such as denial, anger, depression, and bargaining,[2] or working through a more unique process, given the situation. Simply because a victim recognizes that what is owed—a personal or emotional sense of debt—will never be received and has decided to relinquish that debt does not mean that all emotions associated with the loss suddenly dissipate. More than likely, there is going to be some residual anger, sadness, frustration, or other intense emotion that must be dealt with.

Let go of ill will. Realizing that you will not get what you wanted from a person is one thing, but resolving to not feel ill will toward an individual requires additional work. One way to address your feelings might be to acknowledge what the offender might be experiencing. On one hand, the offender might feel guilty, acknowledging what was done that caused harm and being unable to rectify the situation. By relinquishing the debt, the offender might also feel some relief. Relinquishing debt, therefore, might be a way of helping the person who caused the harm. When letting a person off the hook, there can be some residual anger from the victim—as if once again, someone has taken advantage of the situation or even the victim's tendency to give in. On the other hand, an offender may feel nothing at all because this person is no longer present in the life of the victim or because the offender is uncaring. In this situation, the victim is not going to get what was wanted anyway, so holding on to a debt is meaningless and a waste of energy.

Consider these two scenarios. In the first scenario, there is the possibility that relinquishing debt may be perceived as an altruistic act, as discussed in Worthington's model (see Chapter 3).[3] The idea of *just letting someone off the hook* does not accurately describe this action; rather, by letting go of any ill will, both the offender and the victim may experience some relief. In the second scenario, the only consequence of holding onto ill will toward an offender is experienced by the victim. Hence, there is holding onto feelings of righteous indignation or using that energy for something more productive.

Talking through feelings of fear, anger, and depression can be helpful in moving forward and letting go of ill will toward the offender. One goal in this process is to become comfortable with the realization that feelings of ill will serve little benefit to the victim and may in fact be an impediment to either interpersonal or intrapersonal forgiveness. Furthermore, when choosing whether to pursue interpersonal or intrapersonal forgiveness, the victim very likely is forging a new path.

MAKING A DECISION

The decision of whether to pursue interpersonal forgiveness (i.e., reconciling with the offender and renegotiating the relationship) or to choose a path of intrapersonal forgiveness (i.e., mechila, or relinquishing the debt that is owed by the offender and simply moving forward) may involve considering what the future looks like with and without this relationship and the extent to which the existing relationship brings meaning to one's life. Let's consider some facets of this decision.

Termination. Should the relationship be continued or discontinued? Sometimes, relationships are extremely unhealthy but very difficult to terminate, such as when an abuser is also a family member (e.g., a sibling or cousin). We can contrast Sheila's situation with Deanna. In Sheila's case, her father goes to prison for abusing her, but he is eventually released. There may be circumstances, such as family events, when Sheila has to make the decision to avoid contact with her family or risk being in contact with her father. Hence, there are limits to being able to terminate a relationship, but that does not mean that the relationship is reconciled. Sheila does have the option to maintain distance, regardless of the situation. Deanna, on the other hand, was abused by an ex-boyfriend, and she may have the option to totally disconnect from the relationship.

Terminating the relationship is not the only option. In some cases, the victim and offender work toward reconciliation because they see some benefit to working through problems and continuing the relationship. When deciding on whether a relationship should be continued or discontinued, adopting a forgiveness strategy that is based on the severity of the pain experienced by the victim and the level of remorse from the perpetrator might be helpful.[4] Remember, a victim is not under any obligation to reconcile a relationship or offer mechila unless the perpetrator has repented and changed.[5] Although the power and decision to forgive debt or reconcile a relationship belong to the victim, it is the offender who must do the work, show the remorse, and change. At the heart of this process, the person harmed can protect oneself from further abuse.

Reprieve. If it is unlikely that a perpetrator will come to terms with or even admit the harm caused to a victim, the victim still needs to be able to move forward past the event. The victim offers a reprieve from what is owed in order to move forward, with or without the offender. The offender may be forgiven, but that does not imply a reconciled relationship. Key to this process is for the victim to move past resentment. Carrying resentment can be a burden to the victim, especially after a debt, whether tangible or emotional, has been lifted toward the offender. Mechila may be an important concept for the well-being of an individual recovering from the offense. Mechila provides a mechanism to move forward without reconciling with the offender and without feeling encumbered in the future by what is owed.

Helpful. Examining the extent to which a relationship continues to be beneficial is pertinent to deciding between an interpersonal and intrapersonal path. For Jerome and Maria, re-establishing their relationship was important not only for them but also for their kids. On the other hand, re-establishing a relationship between Deanna and her ex-boyfriend could be a harmful endeavor and perhaps a toxic decision. These two scenarios offer two extremes, but it also possible that when a person is recovering from an offense, the experience is somewhere in the middle. When trying to resolve a conflict with someone who has caused harm or pain, there might not be a right or wrong answer, but rather what the person who was harmed perceives as best at this time. Perhaps it is best not to renegotiate a relationship *at this time*, but maybe later. Although the FRM represents a dichotomized choice of interpersonal or intrapersonal forgiveness, the decision to move toward interpersonal or intrapersonal forgiveness does not need to be perceived as permanent but rather as what is best in the present.

Worthwhile. The renegotiation of a relationship can be emotionally taxing, requiring a lot of determination and emotional energy. The decision to renegotiate a relationship should be made because the relationship has value to the person who was harmed. Deciding to renegotiate a relationship, solely for the benefit of the offender, potentially compromises the person who was harmed and could contribute to a pattern of revictimization. Quite simply, renegotiation of a relationship that lacks value to the individual who was harmed should not be pursued.

Sustaining. When relationships have value, they contribute to our overall health and well-being. The establishment of intimacy—close, long-term relationships—is a primary task in adulthood.[6] Consider that many of the relationships in childhood and adolescence are based on activities and environment—who lives in your neighborhood, who attends your school, who participates in similar activities. But beginning in early adulthood, individuals make decisions about relationships based in part on personal qualities as opposed to common experiences. Being thoughtful about the personal impact of a relationship when relationships fail because a person was harmful or acted wrongfully is an important consideration. Rather than simply focusing on the practical aspects of the relationship, considering whether a relationship is healthy and worth sustaining is also important. Although walking away from a previously important relationship may be heartbreaking, attempting to mend something that cannot be fixed is an unhealthy endeavor.

Consequential. The decision to renegotiate a relationship or choose mechila—an intrapersonal approach—requires some forethought into expectations of the relationship and the extent to which the relationship is healthy, empowering, and beneficial. When considering whether a relationship is beneficial, one particular facet to consider is the amount of energy the relationship requires. Ultimately, a recovering victim might ask, "Is this worth it?" Or, "Is this person worth it?" One issue to consider is what I refer to as *vampire relationships*: those relationships that just suck the energy out of us and offer very little in return. Relationships with vampires are draining; they are not sustaining, worthwhile, or helpful. The decision to renegotiate a relationship should be based on mutuality—an equal respect, understanding, and drive to foster and strengthen a relationship that is beneficial to those engaged in the relationship. In Chapter 1, the concept of mutuality—the impact each individual has on the other in a healthy relationship—was introduced. A benefit of a reconciled relationship needs to include a renegotiation of power, and anything short of a mutually empowering, beneficial, and healthy relationship might lead to a more intrapersonal process for the recovering victim.

UNDERSTANDING YOUR JOURNEY

The final phase of the FRM culminates in making a decision about the nature of the relationship between the person who has committed an offense and caused harm and the person who was harmed. Forgiveness, therefore, can be viewed as a conjunctive process whereby a person who was harmed (a) explores feelings related to the injury, (b) reframes the injury by gaining insight into the offensive behavior, and (c) reconciles with the offender. Forgiveness can also be viewed as a disjunctive process, in which the third step is replaced with release or forgiveness of debt, and the individual decreases the negativity associated with the injury without reconciling with the other party. Deciding to relinquish what is owed by the offender but ceasing the relationship does not constitute a failure in the relationship but rather a personal strength in the recovering victim. Moreover, making the decision to renegotiate the relationship is not a weakness of the person who was harmed but rather a desire to reformulate a relationship that is mutually empowering, healthy, and beneficial.

This phase of the FRM is future-oriented, in that you are asked to consider what you think this relationship is going to be like if it continues and how you might deal with the absence of this relationship should it be discontinued. Whether a conjunctive, inter-personal process or a disjunctive, intrapersonal process is pursued, each requires the abandonment of ill will toward the offender. In an interpersonal process, healthy, positive feelings toward the offender are important to renegotiating a mutually empowering, healthy, and beneficial relationship. At the same time, abandoning ill will toward the offender in an intrapersonal process is essential to reducing your emotional burden toward the offender and the situation. Whereas the renegotiation of a relationship can require determination and hard work, so can abandoning ill will and relinquishing what you feel might be owed to you, whether it is tangible (e.g., money, property) or intangible (e.g., closure, an apology). This is where mechila plays an important role in the forgiveness process—by understanding that not all forgiveness requires the other person and that an intrapersonal process can be just as healthy, if not more, in personal recovery.

With each of the four phases of the FRM covered, let's turn our at-tention to a practical strategy for evaluating how individuals may work through the FRM when struggling with issues of conflict and forgive-ness: the Forgiveness Reconciliation Inventory (FRI). In Chapter 8, we will explore how to use this unique tool to understand the forgive-ness process within the context of the four phases of the FRM.

NOTES

1. Balkin et al., 2009.
2. Kübler-Ross, 2005.
3. Wade et al., 2014.
4. Scobie & Scobie, 1998.
5. Blumenthal, 1998.
6. Havighurst, R. J. (1972). *Developmental tasks and education* (3rd ed.). New York: D. McKay.

The Forgiveness
Reconciliation Inventory

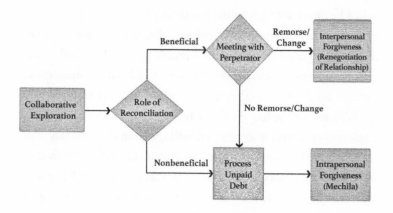

The Forgiveness Reconciliation Model (FRM) helps to provide a way to conceptualize a process toward forgiveness and develop a plan that has a reasonable chance of working for you. But models are only helpful if they are effective and provide some type of underlying truth about what is happening. Numerous models are used in mental health—from how we work through grief, recover from addiction, or develop as human beings. In Chapter 3, the FRM was introduced and compared with other forgiveness models. Subsequent chapters included a description of how each phase of the FRM could be put into practice. But to move a model from a theoretical conceptualization to an evidence-based practice, a mechanism for evaluating how the model may be effective in working through the process of conflict and forgiveness is essential.

The Forgiveness Reconciliation Inventory (FRI; Appendix A) was developed for just this purpose. The FRI is a tool to help individuals work through issues of conflict and forgiveness using the FRM. Hence, the FRI is a tool aligned with the FRM. This chapter includes a description of the FRI and how to administer, score, and interpret the measure for you or someone else. Appendix A provides the FRM. Appendix B includes the psychometric properties of the instrument that mental health workers (e.g., counselors, psychologists, social workers, marriage and family therapists, psychiatrists) often consider when administering, scoring, and interpreting a measure.

The FRI is what I refer to as a *process instrument*. This is not a diagnostic tool. Results from the FRI will not label you as a forgiving person or an unforgiving person. Rather, the FRI provides a representation of where you might fit within each stage of the FRM and provides a visual representation that might confirm or shed some light on thoughts or feelings you are experiencing with a particular situation or person related to conflict and forgiveness. Moreover, the results of the FRI should not be generalized to every situation you experience. Remember, forgiveness is a context-driven process, and the same situation might not have the same personal conclusion given the context. Recall some of our previous examples in which an offense was committed by an acquaintance as opposed to a family member. You might not forgive an acquaintance for stealing money out of your wallet, but you might be more likely to forgive a family member for the same offense because you have to deal with this family member on an ongoing basis and the relationship is much different. Having different rules for various contexts does not make one hypocritical but rather reinforces the human element involved in these relationships. Some relationships can be easily expunged, but others, not so much.

There are two components of the FRI: the items and the scoring profile. As you use the FRI, either because you are (a) a clinician administering this measure to a client, (b) a client having this measure administered to you, or (c) self-administering the FRI, keep the following key points in mind:

1. The FRI is a process instrument. The FRI is used to provide information about where a person might be and some issues to consider within the FRM.
2. The FRI should not be used to diagnose or label an individual.
3. The FRI is context-driven and should be used to help process issues within a single context and not multiple issues that may be handled differently depending on the person and situation.

ADMINISTERING THE FORGIVENESS RECONCILIATION INVENTORY

The FRI is a simple measure to administer and score. The instrument was designed to be administered in the course of counseling by a clinician, but there is nothing overly complex about the administration and scoring that limits the utility of the FRI. Self-administration and scoring are certainly feasible. However, if using this measure for yourself, be cautious about interpretation. Talking through issues of conflict and forgiveness with a licensed clinician can be beneficial and would represent best practice with this measure.

The FRI has four sections. Each section is aligned with one of the four phases of the FRM: collaborative exploration, role of reconciliation, remorse/change, and outcome. There are six items in each section, yielding a total of 24 items. The FRI uses an item type known as *semantic differentials*,[1] in which opposing adjectives are used to describe a phenomenon. In other words, adjectives that are opposites are used to describe various elements of the stages in the FRM. The instructions for the FRI are as follows:

> Think about a time when you were harmed/wronged by someone (if a counselor or caseworker is administering this to you, consider an issue you may be addressing in counseling). How did you feel toward the person? How was your relationship affected?

> Below you will find a statement written in bold and a list of word pairs. Between each word pair are several boxes (□). For the following word pairs, place a ✓ on the appropriate "□" that indicates the extent to which you feel more closely to one of the words. You will have only one "✓" for each word pair.

> *Example:* **Most people are**

> trustworthy ☑ □ □ □ □ untrustworthy

> So, you would check the box above if you felt strongly that most people are trustworthy. The extent to which you feel different could be represented by checking one of the boxes to the right of the present mark.

A statement is offered, followed by six adjective pairs, followed by another statement and six adjective pairs. This process occurs four times for a total of four statements, each aligned with a phase in the FRM, and 24 items. After all 24 items are completed, the FRI is ready to be scored. In addition, pay particular attention to the following in the instructions:

> Think about a time when you were harmed/wronged by someone (if a counselor or caseworker is administering this to you, consider an issue you may be addressing in counseling). How did you feel toward the person? How was your relationship affected?

Notice the previous statement refers to "a time" or "the person." When completing the measure, keeping the frame of reference to a person or single situation is important. Once again, the FRI is used not to identify how forgiving one might be but rather how an individual may address and work through a single situation.

> Place a ✓ on the appropriate "☐" that indicates the extent to which you feel more closely to one of the words for each of the 24 items. You will have only one "✓" for each word pair.

SCORING THE FORGIVENESS RECONCILIATION INVENTORY

After completing all 24 items, the FRI can be scored. Notice that there are five boxes between each adjective pair. The box on the left represents 5. The box on the right represents 1. The boxes in between are 4, 3, and 2 respectively. Using the example given in the instructions, the placement of scores is as follows:

Trustworthy   ☐   ☐   ☐   ☐   ☐   Untrustworthy
               5   4   3   2   1

A mark on the leftmost box next to Trustworthy would be scored 5; a mark next to the rightmost box next to Untrustworthy would be scored 1; a mark in the middle would be scored 3 and represents a more neutral feeling. Scores are recorded for each of the 24 items.

There are four sections of the FRI, each corresponding with a phase or anchor in the FRM:

1. Collaborative Exploration (items 1–6)—*Regarding the person who harmed me, I feel*
2. Role of Reconciliation (items 7–12)—*Re-establishing a relationship with the person who harmed me would be*
3. Remorse/Change (items 13–18)—*The person who harmed me is*
4. Outcome (items 19–24)—*In the future, my relationship with the person who harmed me is likely to be*

After scores are recorded, the scores for items 1 to 6 are summed. This process is repeated for items 7 to 12, 13 to 18, and 19 to 24. Hence, each of the four sections is scored, with scores ranging from 6 to 30. Notice that each of the adjective pairs has a more positive value on the left and a more negative value on the right. Only the summed scores for each of the four sections are taken into account and will be recorded on the FRI Profile (see Appendix A). Simply place a mark by the appropriate number in the first column of the FRI Profile for the summed score on Collaborative Exploration (items 1–6). This process is repeated for the second, third, and fourth columns for the respective phases of Role of Reconciliation (items 7–12), Remorse/Change (items 13–18), and Outcome (items 19–24). This process is demonstrated in the subsequent section along with a summary for completing and scoring the FRI.

1. Place a check mark in one of the boxes. For each section of six items underneath the written statement, add the items. A ✓ in the leftmost box "☐" indicates 5; A ✓ in the rightmost box "☐" indicates 1.
2. Sum each set of six items. Scores will range from 6 to 30. You will have four scores ranging between 6 and 30.
3. In the FRI Profile, there are four columns—one column for each section. Mark an "X" in the first column for the first summed score (items 1–6); the second, third, and fourth summed scores are marked in their respective columns.
4. Draw a line connecting the scores.

UNDERSTANDING THE FORGIVENESS RECONCILIATION INVENTORY PROFILE

The first thing to notice in the scoring profile is that higher scores will represent more positive feelings related to the four statements provided and lower scores will indicate more negative feelings. The FRI is set up so that all the adjectives on the left, aligned with 5, are positive, and all of the adjectives on the right, aligned with 1, are negative. The FRI could theoretically produce 16 profiles, though some of the profiles are not likely to be produced, and the reason will be explained. In the next section, we will explore some common profiles, but this might also be a good time to complete and score the FRI in Appendix A.

Common Profiles

Everything is awesome. The recovering victim views each phase of the FRM in a positive light. Higher scores are noted in each of the four phases (Figure 8.1).

In a scenario such as this, the person who was offended or harmed continues to have positive feelings toward the individual who committed the offense or caused harm, views reconciliation as beneficial, feels that the offender has demonstrated remorse and changed behavior, and sees the renegotiation of the relationship and reconciliation as a meaningful endeavor. Such a scenario might be noted by Jerome and Maria.

No, no, and hell no. In contrast to Figure 8.1, the recovering victim views each phase of the FRM in a negative light. The respondent identifies lower scores in each of the four phases (Figure 8.2).

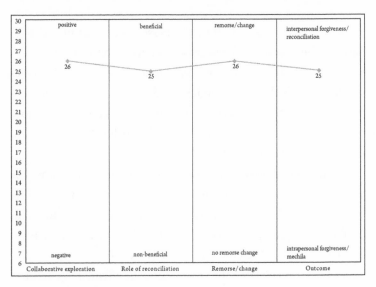

Figure 8.1. Everything is awesome.

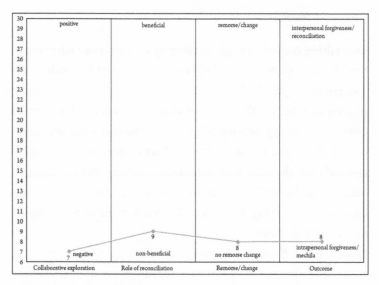

Figure 8.2. No, no, and hell no.

In a scenario such as this, the person who was offended or harmed continues to have negative feelings toward the individual who committed the offense or caused harm, views reconciliation as unhealthy, feels that the offender failed to or is unable to demonstrate any remorse or changed behavior, and sees the need to move forward without the presence of this relationship. Such a scenario might exist for Deanna or Sheila.

I might need to rethink this. This is a more conflicted profile and might be indicative of someone who is putting others before oneself or could even be someone in an abusive relationship. This profile is denoted by low scores in the first three phases of the FRM and a high score in the Outcome phase (Figure 8.3).

In a situation like this, the victim views the offender in a negative light but might feel guilty or compelled to stay in the relationship. The victim acknowledges that the offender is not likely to change

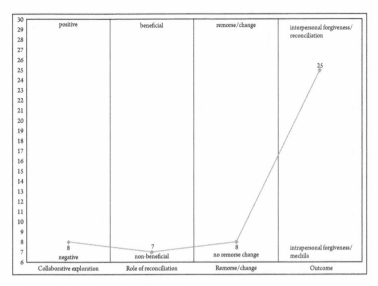

Figure 8.3. I might need to rethink this.

but continues to work toward reconciliation. In all seriousness, this could be a dangerous situation. This type of profile could be indicative of someone who could benefit from counseling and may be typical of individuals who are in an abusive relationship.[2]

I'm not going to get over it. Sometimes, the offender is trying to make things right, but it is too late for the person who was harmed. In this case, the person who is recovering from a transgression might indicate higher scores in the first three phases but a lower score in the Outcome phase (Figure 8.4).

The recovering victim noted positive feelings toward the offender, the benefits of a reconciled relationship, and the remorse/change of the offender. But the recovering victim is not going to get over the offense. Sometimes, this is due to a value-based standard, such as, "I would never stay with someone who cheated on me!" At other times, the recovering victim realizes that no matter how

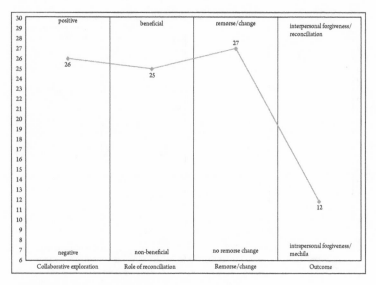

Figure 8.4. I'm not going to get over it.

much they might care about a person, they are not going to get over the hurt or issues of trust. Another possibility is that the recovering victim simply feels indifference toward the offender, indicating that the offender might now be a decent person but simply wants nothing to do with the offender any longer.

I'm trying to see the good in this. Reconciliation can sometimes feel forced, particularly when the victim holds negative feelings toward the offender or questions whether reconciliation is beneficial. In such situations, a person might respond with one of the following profiles:

1. Lower score in Collaborative Exploration and higher scores in the subsequent areas (Figure 8.5)
2. Lower scores in Collaborative Exploration and Role of Reconciliation and higher scores in Remorse/Change and Outcome (Figure 8.6).

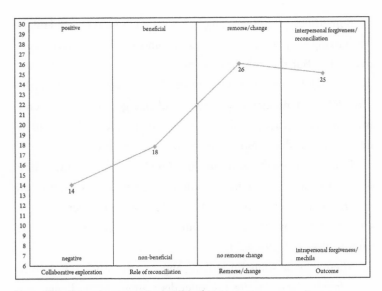

Figure 8.5. I'm trying to see the good in this.

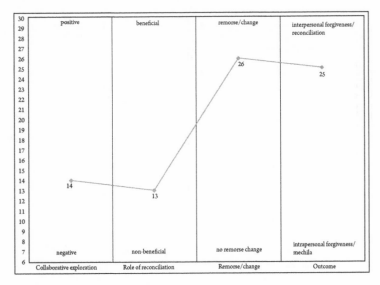

Figure 8.6. I'm trying to see the good in this.

Sometimes, you are just angry. A person who was harmed might be thinking (or perhaps being told by someone else), "I need to get over this!" But the individual is not "just getting over it." Rather, even though the victim might see some benefit to reconciliation, the offender has demonstrated remorse and change, and there is some movement toward reconciliation, the residual anger still needs to be dealt with in order to move forward in a healthy way.

I just can't see the good in this. Simply because reconciliation is beneficial and the offender is intent on changing does not mean that reconciliation is going to occur. Here, we see lower scores in Collaborative Exploration and Outcome but higher scores in the middle phases (Figure 8.7).

There may be some underlying anger or dissatisfaction toward the offender, and despite the offender's attempts to change, the recovering victim simply does not see the benefit or the value in

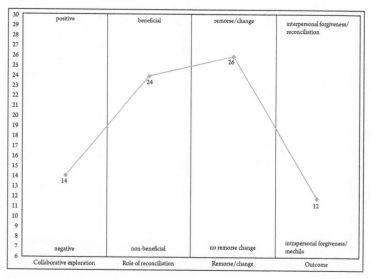

Figure 8.7. I just can't see the good in this.

pursuing reconciliation and chooses to move forward without the relationship.

Not going to change, and this is unhealthy. This is a more conflicted profile and might be indicative of someone who is putting others before oneself or could even be someone in an abusive relationship. This profile (Figure 8.8) is noted by alternating low and high scores in each of the four phases.

Similar to the *I might need to rethink this* profile in Figure 8.3, the victim views the offender in a negative light but might consider staying in the relationship for external reasons or pressure, perhaps because of cultural expectations, fear of change, fear of the offender, or belief that some greater good might come out of the relationship (e.g., not disappointing kids or family). The victim acknowledges that the offender is not likely to change but continues to work toward reconciliation.

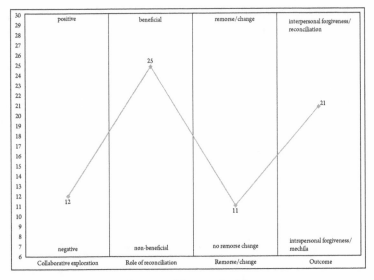

Figure 8.8. Not going to change, and this is unhealthy.

This is toxic, but I like it. Yes, this happens too. Unhealthy tendencies might be noted when higher scores are evident in Collaborative Exploration and Outcome, but lower scores are indicated in Role of Reconciliation and Remorse/Change (Figure 8.9). This profile is the opposite of *I just can't see the good in this* (see Figure 8.7).

Sometimes, ending an unhealthy relationship is difficult because there may be aspects of it that are enjoyable. Even if the relationship is abusive, there may also be some dependency issues or addiction. Individuals with this type of profile might benefit from counseling because the offender is unlikely to change, and the victim might have a tendency toward unhealthy relationships.

Not ending over this. In a scenario such as this, the recovering victim is inclined toward reconciliation, perhaps because the offense is not severe enough to result in terminating a relationship, or

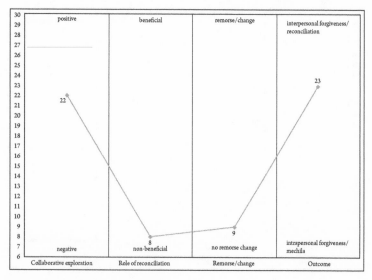

Figure 8.9. This is toxic, but I like it.

the recovering is not just not at the point that the relationship has no value, even if the offender has not changed. Elevated scores are denoted except in Remorse/Change (Figure 8.10).

The victim of the offense in this case should be cautious because of the potential for a power differential in which the offender has more power in the relationship owing to the victim's stronger investment in the relationship.

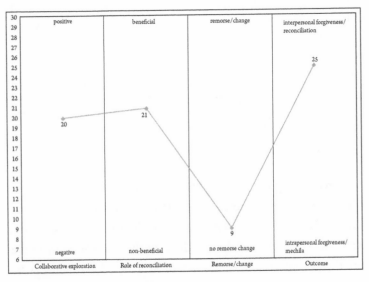

Figure 8.10. Not ending over this.

I'm just not into it. Sometimes, feelings change toward a remorseful offender. Even if the relationship was positive, reconciliation after being hurt can be difficult. In such cases, a victim might identify positive feelings toward the offender and the belief that the offender has changed, but denote less benefit to reconciliation (Figure 8.11). An interesting feature is that this profile is the opposite of *Not going to change, and this is unhealthy* (see Figure 8.8).

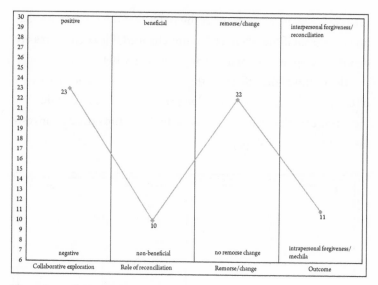

Figure 8.11. I'm just not into it.

A recovering victim may simply wish to move on without the complications of the relationship. Rebuilding trust can be hard work and needs to be perceived as worthwhile. For reasons that will be discussed in the next chapter, this is likely an uncommon profile, and the Role of Reconciliation is unlikely to be a determining factor in the decision to pursue an interpersonal or intrapersonal path of forgiveness.

I'm kind of into it. Occasionally, we become involved in relationships with individuals who are not healthy for us, or we may not be particularly good for them. And even though we recognize this, we still engage in the relationship. So, we experience positive feelings toward the offender but recognize that reconciliation is not beneficial; yet, the offender has changed and expressed

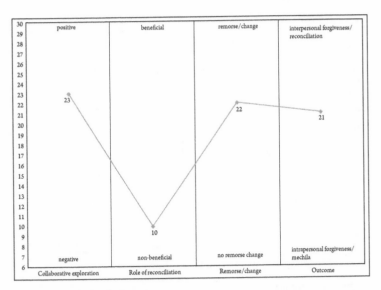

Figure 8.12. I'm kind of into it.

remorse, and we feel drawn to re-engage in the relationship (Figure 8.12).

This could turn out to be an unhealthy scenario, so an individual with this profile may want to proceed cautiously if the decision is to reconcile the relationship.

Just no. In many situations, reconciliation is just not going to happen. These profiles (Figures 8.13, 8.14, 8.15 and 8.16) follow a similar theme to Figure 8.2, *No, no, and hell no*. However, at least one score in the first three phases is elevated.

Each of these scenarios leads to a similar outcome of pursuing an intrapersonal forgiveness path. Although the recovering victim is able to see some elements of the offender in a positive light, the remaining elements point to reconciliation being less likely and perhaps even unhealthy in some cases.

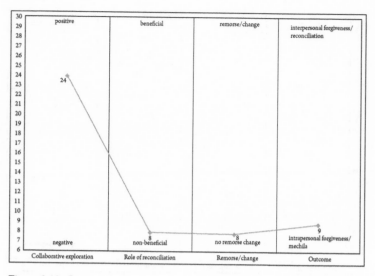

Figure 8.13. Just no.

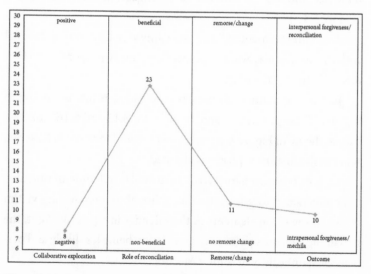

Figure 8.14. Just no.

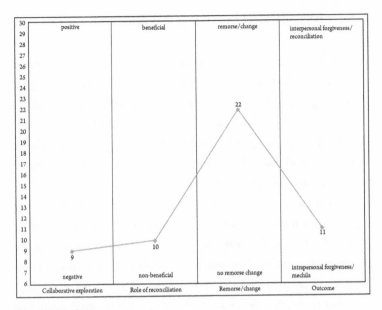

Figure 8.15. Just no.

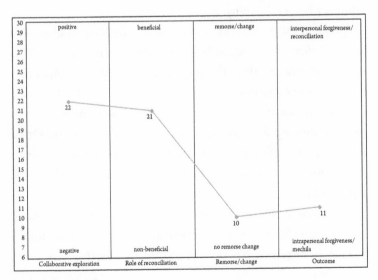

Figure 8.16. Just no.

UNDERSTANDING YOUR JOURNEY

Although not every scenario was covered, there is a strong likelihood that your scores are similar to one of the 16 profiles. Remember that these are general profiles, and there can be specific nuances with respect to some scores being slightly more elevated. One scenario not discussed is a profile that is neutral all the way across. You could be numb to everything, which probably indicates that you have more work to do and are not ready to make a decision.

Perhaps one of the benefits of this measure is getting a visual representation of where you are in the process of addressing conflict and forgiveness within a specific situation. Sometimes, seeing the results might confirm how you feel regarding the offense or the offender and can provide some clarity to the path you are considering. At other times, you might see that your profile is rather conflicted or there is a need for you reflect further or work with a counselor to address what is happening.

Some of the profiles discussed in this chapter might illuminate areas we often avoid, such as *This is toxic, but I like it* (see Figure 8.9) or *I might need to rethink this* (see Figure 8.3). These profiles may represent situations in which talking to someone you trust, seeking feedback, or obtaining professional help can be informative and valuable to working through issues of conflict and forgiveness. Other times, a profile can be an indicator of your rational or instinctive feeling about how to move forward (e.g., *No, no, and hell no;* see Figure 8.2).

Scores on the FRI tend to be accurate with respect to pinpointing how an individual is working through the FRM. The FRI is a unique tool or strategy that has been shown to be effective as a counseling interventions when working with individuals struggling or addressing issues of conflict and forgiveness.[3] In Chapter 9, we will go over the some of the benefits of and evidence for this strategy.

NOTES

1. Osgood, C. E., Suci, G., & Tannenbaum, P. (1957). *The measurement of meaning*. Urbana: University of Illinois Press.
2. Balkin et al., 2014.
3. Harris, N. A. (2015). *Using the forgiveness and reconciliation inventory: A qualitative inquiry examining the experiences of the process* (Order No. 3736191). Available from ProQuest Dissertations & Theses A&I. (1747126493). Retrieved from http://umiss.idm.oclc.org/login?url=https://search-proquest-com.umiss.idm.oclc.org/docview/1747126493?accountid=14588

Chapter 9

Does This Work?

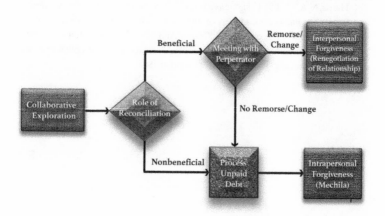

Perhaps one of the most important issues within the mental health field is whether what we do actually works for our clients. There are thousands of theories, strategies, and techniques within the mental health field. Some of these fall into the category of sham therapies, such as rebirthing therapy, conversion therapy, and emotional freedom techniques. The process of ethical, methodical, and rigorous research to support the use of strategies such as the Forgiveness Reconciliation Model (FRM) and the Forgiveness Reconciliation Inventory (FRI) is important for the mental health disciplines. Whereas Appendix B provides a summary of the psychometric properties of the FRI, in this chapter, we cover some research into the FRI and FRM and why this might a good approach to addressing issues of conflict and forgiveness.

Recall from Chapter 3 that models are a way to conceptualize a process and develop a plan that has a reasonable chance of working. Models serve as a framework. They provide a way to move forward in a process that may keep individuals on track if they get lost. They also provide a way to understand problems and issues and work through them. Models may illustrate a journey and help form meaning in the process.

But a model should extend beyond an idea or conceptual framework. A good model should be substantiated through research that is empirical and scientific and through narrative inquiry—a process known as *qualitative research* that uses personal experiences identified through interviews, observations, and document collection to identify themes of experiences related to what is being studied. Throughout this book, numerous research studies related to forgiveness have been cited, and the importance of addressing forgiveness appears to be well-founded with respect to enhancing mental health and well-being. In addition, there is compelling evidence that the FRM and the FRI, a measure of the FRM, work together as a helpful intervention to address issues of conflict and forgiveness. For those interested in a more technical description of these issues, please refer to Table 9.1 and Appendix B, which provides an overview of research studies related to the FRM and FRI.

WHAT WE HAVE LEARNED FROM STUDYING OTHERS

Take a look at the FRM at the top of the chapter (and yes, I am aware that this model has appeared at the beginning of almost all

Table 9.1 PUBLICATIONS RELATED TO THE FORGIVENESS RECONCILIATION
MODEL AND THE FORGIVENESS RECONCILIATION INVENTORY

Author (Year)	Title	Publication	Summary
Balkin, R. S., Freeman, S. J., & Lyman, S. R. (2009)	Forgiveness, reconciliation, and mechila: Integrating the Jewish concept of forgiveness in to clinical practice	Counseling and Values, Vol. 53	Provides an overview of the Forgiveness Reconciliation Model
Balkin, R. S., Harris, N., Freeman, S. J., & Huntington, S. (2014)	The Forgiveness Reconciliation Inventory: An instrument to process through issues of forgiveness and conflict	Measurement and Evaluation in Counseling and Development, Vol. 47	Describes the development and valid use of the Forgiveness Reconciliation Inventory
Balkin, R. S., Perepiczka, M., Sowell, S. M., Cumi, K., & Gnilka, P. G. (2016)	The Forgiveness-Reconciliation Model: An empirically supported process for humanistic counseling	Journal of Humanistic Counseling, Vol. 55	Provides empirical support for the Forgiveness Reconciliation Model through the use of the Forgiveness Reconciliation Inventory
Harris, N. A. (2015)	Using the forgiveness and reconciliation inventory: A qualitative inquiry examining the experiences of the process	Available from ProQuest Dissertations & Theses A&I	Clinicians and clients were interviewed after working through the Forgiveness Reconciliation Model and using the Forgiveness Reconciliation Inventory.

of the chapters, and you might be tired of looking at it). The FRM provides a sequential approach to addressing issues of conflict and forgiveness and uses the framework of a flow chart to illustrate this sequence. Hence, there is a beginning phase, a decision phase, and an end phase that is dependent on the previous phases. One way to demonstrate the effectiveness of a model is to show evidence that how one starts the model and works through each phase is predictive of where one ends up—whether the individual pursues reconciliation or mechila.

What Really Matters

In a study published in 2016, I and my colleagues evaluated 200 participants who took the FRI and found that where an individual starts in the first phase of collaborative exploration is predictive of the outcome phase—the choice between reconciliation and mechila.[1] In other words, individuals who reported more positive feelings toward the offender in the collaborative exploration phase were more likely to choose to reconcile the relationship; individuals who reported less positive feelings toward the offender in the collaborative exploration phase were more likely to choose an intrapersonal forgiveness path. But that doesn't tell the whole story because, if that was the case, we could just examine how people felt toward the offender and encourage them to move toward interpersonal or intrapersonal forgiveness based on that limited information. What really seemed to influence people beyond where they started was what happens in the middle phases—processing the role of reconciliation and examining the extent to which the offender expressed remorse and changed behavior. Both of these middle phases serve as the crux of the FRM. Having positive feelings toward someone who has caused harm, pain, or discomfort might seem like a strong predictor of reconciliation but could be mediated by knowing that such a reconciliation might be unhealthy or that the offender really does not show much remorse or change. The antithesis might also be true. An individual who harbors negative feelings toward an offender might be influenced to reconcile if reconciliation is viewed as beneficial or if the offender demonstrates remorse and change. Such a scenario may seem unlikely but could fall into scenarios previous discussed in which the victim feels pressure to reconcile or believes the negative feelings toward the offender may dissipate over time.

Internal and external processes play a role in forgiveness. Keep in mind that the second phase of the FRM, role of reconciliation, is an internal process, and the third phase of the FRM, remorse/change, is an external process. How one feels about whether reconciliation is beneficial is a decision the victim addresses; the decision for an offender to express remorse and change behavior is outside of the scope of the person harmed. Once again, the outcome of this process is likely influenced by the initial feelings the victim has toward the offender and the offender's openness to change.

Because the role of reconciliation phase represents a more internal process, becoming more aware of what you want and the expectations you have are important considerations, whether attempting to renegotiate a relationship or deciding to move forward without the relationship but still relinquishing feelings of ill will toward the offender. Because the FRM is a sequential model, considering and understanding the role of reconciliation can be important to addressing issues that arise in the outcome phase. In addition, processing the role of reconciliation has been supported in past research[2] and appears to be important to enhancing relationships. Seeking help from a trusted person, mentor, or counselor[3] during this phase, can foster change and growth when recovering from hurt, pain, and trauma.[4] But, even if an individual endorses positive feelings and views reconciliation as beneficial, the remorse and change of the offender are also a pertinent mediator and may influence the outcome toward an intrapersonal process. Simply put, reconciliation is difficult, and often unhealthy, when the offending individual shows no intention of remorse and change.

Healthy Individuals May Know When to Let Go or Renegotiate the Relationship

Of the 200 individuals that were studied, 69 (34.5%) were receiving counseling services within correctional settings, outpatient women's recovery centers, and domestic abuse shelters. So, how were individuals who were receiving counseling different from those who were not involved with counseling services? Perhaps not surprisingly, individuals who were in counseling were more likely to identify negative attributes toward the person who caused them harm or pain and were more likely to address forgiveness from an intrapersonal perspective. In other words, individuals in counseling identified fewer benefits of reconciliation and less likelihood that the offender demonstrated any remorse and change. Individuals not receiving mental health services were more likely to renegotiate a relationship with the person who harmed them. What is also worth pointing out is that regardless of whether someone was in counseling, individuals had similar feelings about the person who harmed them—only their views about reconciliation and the extent to which the offender was remorseful were different. So, what does all of this mean?

1. People who do not seek counseling services might view forgiveness as an interpersonal process and only consider the renegotiation of the relationship as conducive to forgiveness. They may also have less severe breaches in the relationship.

2. Individuals who seek counseling might be more likely to view forgiveness from an intrapersonal lens. They also tend to view their offender and the relationship in a more negative light.

3. One reason for seeking counseling could be the severity of the relationship; hence, individuals seek counseling because they recognize that the person who hurt them is not remorseful or willing to change.

4. Counseling may be helpful to explore intrapersonal aspects of forgiveness and mechila.

The Forgiveness Reconciliation Inventory Is a Good Measure of the Stages in the Forgiveness Reconciliation Model

Much of the research mentioned previously comes from studies using the FRI, an instrument aligned with the FRM. So what? Aren't all measures aligned with theory? Actually, no. There are a number of popular measures that were developed without theory or adapted to theory long after development. For example, when intelligence tests were first developed in the early 1900s by Alfred Binet, the goal was to evaluate mental ability in children to identify those who may not be successful in traditional educational environments because of educational deficits. At this time, there was no agreed-on definition of intelligence, but this did not stop individuals such as Henry Goddard, who in 1908 was tasked with administering translated versions of Binet's scale to immigrants at Ellis Island. Goddard was a champion of eugenics and wrongly believed that immigrants would contribute to the decline in intelligence and the white race in the United States. These beliefs resulted in the segregation and discrimination of immigrants when they arrived in the United States. Much later in the 20th century, intelligence measures would be revised, taking into account theoretical underpinnings of intelligence.[5]

The same critique can also be made about some popular psychological measures, such as the Minnesota Multiphasic Personality Inventory (MMPI) and its later iterations, which was initially developed to identify differences in people diagnosed with psychopathology from the normal population. Hence, items such as "I like mechanics magazines" did not theoretically align with any particular disorder but did tend to differentiate those diagnosed with a psychiatric disorder. Such practice in instrument development can be dangerous, especially when misused, as seen with the case of Henry Goddard.

So, developing an instrument that is aligned with a recognized theory is an important consideration to protect the public who might use a measure to help gain insight into difficult issues that might not be discussed with another person. In addition, the FRI was essential to explaining the sequence and use of the FRM, showing that the logical progression of the model assisted people who struggle with issues of conflict and forgiveness to work through feelings of ill will toward an offender, empowering themselves in their recovery.

The Forgiveness Reconciliation Inventory Is Similar to Other Forgiveness Measures, but Also Different

As discussed in Chapter 3, the FRM is not the only forgiveness model, and the FRI is not the only forgiveness measure. Rye and colleagues published two measures of forgiveness in 2001: the Forgiveness Scale and the Forgiveness Likelihood Scale.[6]

The Forgiveness Scale was similar to the FRI in that it was "designed to measure forgiveness toward a particular offender."[7] Higher scores on this scale reflected greater forgiveness toward an offender. In this scale, intrapersonal forgiveness was not considered. In a study of 170 participants who were administered the FRI and Forgiveness Scale, we found that participants who were more likely to forgive on the Forgiveness Scale also were more likely to endorse an interpersonal process on the FRI.

The Forgiveness Likelihood Scale provided 10 scenarios of wrongdoing, such as a significant other having a one-night stand or a friend starting a nasty rumor about you that is untrue, and the respondent is asked to rate, on a scale of 1 (*not at all likely*) to 5 (*extremely likely*), the likelihood of forgiving the person who committed the transgression. The FRI was not designed to identify the extent to which an individual is a forgiving person, so there was less commonality with this measure. Nevertheless, a higher likelihood to forgive was associated with stronger tendencies toward interpersonal forgiveness on the FRI.

The FRI, therefore, shared similarities to Rye's scales but also added elements to differentiate from them by evaluating intrapersonal forgiveness. In addition, Rye's measures were developed as part of a study involving women in college who were wronged in a previous romantic relationship, whereas the FRI included a broader group of participants and no specific requirements about experiencing being wronged.

What Do People Say Who Use the Forgiveness Reconciliation Model and Forgiveness Reconciliation Inventory?

I realize this sounds very technical, so it might be helpful to identify what individuals actually say when working with the model. In 2015, Nephaterria Harris, PhD, conducted individual interviews and a focus group with five adult participants working through issues of conflict and forgiveness in therapy, using the FRM, and taking the FRI. The participants in this narrative inquiry identified becoming more self-aware about their own feelings and conflicts about forgiveness and the process of forgiveness. Individuals had "a better understanding of forgiveness and where they were in the process of forgiving others, as well as needing or wanting forgiveness from others." The visualization of the scores was also helpful in providing a synopsis of strengths and challenges in relationships as well as conflicts. Participants noted that the scores on the FRI were an accurate reflection of their feelings related to forgiveness and reconciliation at the moment. So, not only was the FRI accurate from a perspective of measurement used in social science research, but it also shed light on specific elements of the participants' forgiveness journey. One individual who had struggled with past abuse said the following after seeing scores and working through the process with a counselor:

> It mainly helped me realize . . . where I am with all of the abuse . . . it isn't as overwhelming as it was 20 years ago . . . it is still there, and will always probably be there . . . I can work on it.

In addition, participants noted that the focus on the intrapersonal aspects of forgiveness provided a way to stop avoiding painful events and address them in a safe and meaningful way.[8]

Dr. Harris also interviewed six counselors who used the FRM and FRI with their clients. They noted that the process was useful for clients in understanding themselves and others in order to address healthy relationships or remove themselves from unhealthy relationships. Moreover, using the FRI often highlighted unresolved issues, which affected the emotional content of the session. The process was viewed as beneficial, but at times clients may be emotional.[9]

Overall, individuals found the process beneficial, but issues of conflict and forgiveness can be intense. This is another reason to reflect on the collaborative exploration phase of the FRM. Working through intense emotions can be difficult, and having someone for support and feedback may be beneficial. Sharing such a journey may be safer and more helpful in the long run.

UNDERSTANDING YOUR JOURNEY

When you reflect on your journey, you might consider how your understanding of forgiveness has evolved. Maybe you have found a path toward reconciliation and renegotiating a relationship. Or, perhaps you recognize that a relationship is not salvageable, healthy, or possible to reconcile, so your focus has been on the idea that in order to move forward, you need to relinquish feelings of ill will toward the offender, with no obligation toward the perpetrator who caused harm or pain. Because forgiveness is most easily conceptualized as a relational process between people, it is this intrapersonal process— mechila—that is often more challenging. A relational process has the advantage of at least two people working toward a shared goal of reconciliation. But in an intrapersonal process, it's you—and anyone else with whom you share this journey.

The FRM might be different because of its emphasis on both interpersonal and intrapersonal processes. By attending to your story, either through individual contemplation or sharing with another trusted person, you eventually settle on a path toward interpersonal or intrapersonal forgiveness. Sometimes, this path is not so straightforward. There can be conflict regarding how you feel toward the person who caused harm or pain and the importance of the relationship. While you have some say in your feelings toward the offender, you likely have less control regarding the willingness of the offender to change. Difficulty in forgiveness is sometimes related not only to your feelings regarding the relationship but also to what is realistic. Pursuing reconciliation with a remorseless perpetrator can be dangerous and unhealthy. Withdrawing from a relationship can be painful and a source of grief. This is why forgiveness is a process—a journey. Take your time. Be gentle with yourself.

Throughout this book, we have used the stories of Sheila, Deanna, Jerome and Maria, and Derek to show what working through the various stages of the FRM might look like. You might be frustrated that I have not disclosed the end of these stories with a nice, thorough conclusion. These stories are still evolving. Just because the relationships have been reconciled or have ended does not mean they are not reconsidered. There is no forgetting what transpired between Jerome and Maria, but there is the recognition of growth. Deanna might move on from the very unhealthy relationship she experienced and choose to reflect on her growth, but the trauma of what transpired may still rear its ugly head from time to time. When it does, she has her experience and wisdom to deal with it. Derek never gets the reconciled relationship he desired with his mom. She passed away and never returned the affection he desired. He must learn to free himself of the expectations of the relationship. In this case, the intrapersonal path is not a choice—it is the only option. And then there is Sheila, whose story was a chief inspiration behind the FRM. She must work through cultural expectations, trauma, abuse, and neglect from multiple sources. And if she continues to have contact with her family, she must find a way to balance the intrapersonal process of forgiveness with the potential for continued conflict with family members. Sheila's story may be ongoing with continued challenges and growth.

Beyond serving as an example of the FRM stages, these stories serve as a memorable way to convey meaning from experiences, such as trauma and suffering, and foster perseverance and healing. Storytelling may be "the primary means by which we communicate with others, make sense of our experiences, and hold onto our memories that are most significant."[10] This was an important facet to the first phase of the FRM, collaborative exploration, when the sharing of the offense that transpired promotes thoughtful processing and healing. The development of the FRM was based on the counseling relationship and the sharing of stories. Perhaps, therefore, it is fundamental that the journey of working through conflict and forgiveness is shared. Everybody has a story. The FRM provides a way to share your story and understand your journey. This is a universal journey. Everyone experiences it at some level, and there is healing in sharing it.

NOTES

1. Balkin et al., 2016.
2. Enright et al. 1998.
3. Balkin et al., 2009.
4. Duncan, 2014.
5. Balkin, R. S., & Juhnke, G. A. (2018). *Assessment in counseling: Practice and applications.* New York: Oxford University Press.
6. Rye, M. S., Loiacono, D. M., Folck, C. D., Olszewski, B. T., Heim, T. A., & Madia, B. P. (2001). Evaluation of the psychometric properties of two forgiveness scales. *Current Psychology, 20,* 260–277.
7. Balkin et al., 2014, p. 5.
8. Harris, 2015, pp. 49–51.
9. Ibid.
10. Kottler, J. A. (2018). The power of storytelling to promote resilience and recovery from life's disappointments and tragedies (p. 4). *Televizion.* Retrieved on August 15, 2019, from https://www.br-online.de/jugend/izi/english/publication/televizion/31_2018_E/Kottler-The_power_of_storytelling.pdf

EPILOGUE

I ended the final chapter without a definitive conclusion of the stories used throughout the book. I discussed the importance of stories and conjectured about what may or may not transpire in each individual's journey. In all honesty, I also wonder about my own resistance to placing a tidy bow on these stories. Was it due to exhaustion? Laziness? A lack of creativity?

I am generally not a lazy person. In fact, I am quite the opposite. In attempting to ask myself about whether these stories should have a conclusion or should be left as is, I considered my thoughts about trauma.

Each of these stories has a traumatic component, some cases perhaps more severe than others. Derek's loss of his mother without closure cannot be ignored. The abuse suffered by Deanna and Sheila was severe. And the distrust sown between Jerome and Maria is difficult to reconcile. Does forgiveness, whether interpersonal or intrapersonal, really result in closure?

A common anecdote when relationships end is for a person to say, "I just want closure." It's as if there is some conversation that might transpire that would suddenly end all anxiety and provide relief and a finality to the situation. More than likely, even if such a conversation were to occur, such a moment would be filled with anxiety, and we would all probably walk away thinking, "Damn, I wish I would have said _____!" or "Why didn't I say _____?" Opportunities for closure often do not hit the mark, and even if they do, we sometimes revisit these moments or continue to be haunted by them.

In Chapter 3, I shared a personal story about my bicycle accident. I was hit by a pickup truck, and the person who hit me stayed with me, even holding my hand, as the ambulance arrived. He shed tears and told the police officer, "I did not see him." I never got the closure I wanted. I sought out the driver, hoping to share a beer with him, but was never able to reach him. Admittedly, I do not have any regrets about the situation. I have no anger toward the driver. In fact, it is quite the opposite. One of my most clear memories about that entire incident is being on the ground and the driver grasping my hand. It's the human connection!

But from time to time, I revisit this scene in my mind. I feel it— not every time but on occasion when a car passes me. I get a chill. I have butterflies in my stomach. I feel it in my body. Goosebumps appear all over my arms. I anxiously look to my left (it's usually on my left because I mostly drive or ride in the slow lane) and watch the car pass. It seems like forever. I remind myself that this is a trauma response. I am not in danger, but yet the anxiety is real. At the time of this writing, the bicycle accident was 13 years ago. But it is still with me—even though I have forgiven. I still revisit the trauma, even though I have forgiven. There is no tidy bow on the story. But I am well, and I am not angry.

Of course, this was just an accident. And it affected me, not someone I love. As repeated often in the book, forgiveness is context-driven, and each situation should be treated as unique.

A FUNNY THING HAPPENED ON THE WAY
TO WRITING A BOOK ABOUT FORGIVENESS

During the writing of this book, I had a completely new challenge. It started out rather innocuously—my wife was to have a routine, outpatient procedure to remove an ovarian cyst and ovary. We were told to anticipate a 2-day recovery at home. She had the procedure, and after 2 days, she still appeared to be in considerable pain. After 3 days, there was no change, and the discomfort seemed worse. By day 4, she had vomited. On day 6, she vomited again and was having severe abdominal pain. We ended up in the emergency department on Sunday afternoon.

The emergency department was horrible. My wife was in considerable pain, and they were trying to start an intravenous line but to no avail. It took multiple attempts, and she was crying. I sobbed, too, as this was going on. It was difficult to watch. Within 3 hours of getting to the emergency department, she was in surgery. It turns out that during the procedure to remove the ovarian cyst and ovary, her small intestine was perforated. This was the source of the ongoing complications. The small intestine was repaired, and she was admitted to intensive care unit (ICU). As I was waiting to visit her in the ICU, the surgeon came out to talk to me about the surgery. He told me about the injury that occurred during the first surgery, how it was repaired, and then said, "Every surgeon makes mistakes. If a surgeon has told you they have never made a mistake, they are lying to you."

At this point I am still in shock, just taking in what has transpired and learning what has been done. As a result of the surgery, there would be an open wound, and she would be hooked up to a wound vac. I did not understand what a wound vac was or the type of care that would be needed.

As I was still waiting to see my wife, it was around 8:30 p.m. on a Sunday evening, the surgeon who performed the initial surgery to remove the cyst and ovary came to the waiting area. He apologized to me. "I am so sorry." It was appropriate and heartfelt. We talked a little bit. I do not recall much of the conversation. But he did come to visit us in the hospital, and he did apologize to my wife. The severity of the situation eventually began to hit. My wife was in a lot of pain. This pain would continue for weeks. She had drainage tubes. She was hospitalized for a week and discharged on a wound vac. We were preparing to celebrate our 25th wedding anniversary and take an Alaskan cruise. That was gone. There would be medical bills. The kids would be scared for their mother. They cried, wondering if their mom would get better. I assured them she would, but this was a long haul. I was focused on my wife's recovery, but at some point, I would need to return to the surgery—a physician made an error that had a severe effect on my wife, and had it not been caught, she could have died.

During the process of writing this book, I have been involved in the making of two documentaries with my friend, John Afamasaga, who is also a filmmaker. Always playing the provocative devil's advocate, John said to me, "This is America. This is Suit Nation. He deserves this (to be sued)."

Who am I to say what people deserve? Maybe this surgeon has been practicing for more than 30 years. How many lives do you save in that time? And then you make a mistake. Does it erase all the good you have done, all the lives that have been saved? What if suddenly, after all these years of saving people, this surgeon now questions his ability and skill or has self-doubts? Indeed, we all make mistakes.

I know that feeling. In my field of counseling, studies on client suicide are rare. One of the few studies about client suicide while under the care of a counselor was conducted in 2000 by Charles

McAdams III and Victoria Foster.[1] They estimated that approximately one in four counselors will experience a client suicide. I'm one of those four. I was not sued.

What does this surgeon deserve? Maybe he deserves grace. I don't know. At the time of this writing, my wife is still receiving wound care, but she is expected to make a full recovery. I have three healthy daughters, a nice house, and a great job. In less than a year from now, we will probably take that Alaskan cruise we had to cancel. We will probably reflect on this experience, and maybe even talk about how miserable it was. Sometimes, my wife and I are still angry. This sucked. But there is nothing vengeful. There is no ill will wished on anyone. There is no debt that can be repaid. It is mechila—what we wanted, a healthy outcome from a routine surgery, was not what we got, and we missed out on a lot of things. My wife experienced a lot of pain and trauma, both physical and emotional. What was taken cannot be given back, but we can move on and be at peace with what occurred.

I never meant for this book to be about me. But one of my former professors, Dr. Christopher Lucas, said during a final class, "The job of a professor is to profess." At the beginning of this epilogue, I indicated there is no tidy bow I could tie on the stories shared in this book. There is not a tidy bow for my story either. Forgiveness is indeed a journey. I wish for you and those you help along the way nothing but peace on your journey.

NOTE

1. McAdams, C. A., & Foster, V. A. (2000). Client suicide: Its frequency and impact on counselors. *Journal of Mental Health Counseling, 22,* 107. doi:10.1002/j.1556-6978.1999.tb01787.x

---

The Forgiveness Reconciliation Inventory

Think about a time when you were harmed/wronged by someone (if a counselor or caseworker is administering this to you, consider an issue you may be addressing in counseling). How did you feel toward the person? How was your relationship affected?

Below you will find a statement written in bold and a list of word pairs. Between each word pair are several boxes (□). For the following word pairs, place a ✓ on the appropriate "□" that indicates the extent to which you feel more closely to one of the words. You will have only one "✓" for each word pair.

Example: **Most people are**

trustworthy   ☑   □   □   □   □   untrustworthy

So, you would check the box above if you felt strongly that most people are trustworthy. The extent to which you feel differently could be represented by checking one of the boxes to the right of the present mark.

A. **Regarding the person who harmed me, I feel**

1. peaceful	□	□	□	□	□ hostile
2. nurtured	□	□	□	□	□ abused
3. well-treated	□	□	□	□	□ exploited
4. content	□	□	□	□	□ dissatisfied
5. passive	□	□	□	□	□ aggressive
6. affection	□	□	□	□	□ hatred

B. **Re-establishing a relationship with the person who harmed me would be**

7. helpful	☐	☐	☐	☐	☐	harmful
8. generous	☐	☐	☐	☐	☐	selfish
9. selfless	☐	☐	☐	☐	☐	inconsiderate
10. compassionate	☐	☐	☐	☐	☐	unfeeling
11. empathic	☐	☐	☐	☐	☐	indifferent
12. sensible	☐	☐	☐	☐	☐	careless

C. **The person who harmed me is**

13. remorseful	☐	☐	☐	☐	☐	unapologetic
14. modest	☐	☐	☐	☐	☐	shameless
15. changed	☐	☐	☐	☐	☐	unaltered
16. honest	☐	☐	☐	☐	☐	deceitful
17. principled	☐	☐	☐	☐	☐	manipulative
18. ethical	☐	☐	☐	☐	☐	immoral

D. **In the future, my relationship with the person who harmed me is likely to be**

19. continued	☐	☐	☐	☐	☐	discontinued
20. pardoned	☐	☐	☐	☐	☐	resented
21. beneficial	☐	☐	☐	☐	☐	useless
22. pursued	☐	☐	☐	☐	☐	avoided
23. healthy	☐	☐	☐	☐	☐	unwell
24. meaningful	☐	☐	☐	☐	☐	worthless

FRI Profile

Exploration positive	Role beneficial	Change remorse/change	Outcome interpersonal forgiveness/reconciliation
30	30	30	30
29	29	29	29
28	28	28	28
27	27	27	27
26	26	26	26
25	25	25	25
24	24	24	24
23	23	23	23
22	22	22	22
21	21	21	21
20	20	20	20
19	19	19	19
18	18	18	18
17	17	17	17
16	16	16	16
15	15	15	15
14	14	14	14
13	13	13	13
12	12	12	12
11	11	11	11
10	10	10	10
9	9	9	9
8	8	8	8
7	7	7	7
6	6	6	6
Negative	Non-beneficial	No remorse/change	Intrapersonal forgiveness/mechila

Psychometric Properties of the Forgiveness Reconciliation Inventory

The following information is a summary of the research studies conducted with the Forgiveness Reconciliation Inventory (FRI) and the Forgiveness Reconciliation Model (FRM). Table 9.1 (see Chapter 9) provides an overview of the published research at the time of this writing. The validation of the FRI is based on a comprehensive review of the literature related to forgiveness (see Balkin et al., 2009, 2014) and series of analyses using a representative sample of 200 participants from a variety of clinical and nonclinical settings, including professionals from a community-based education program ($N = 131$, 65.5%) and participants receiving services in correctional settings, outpatient recovery centers, and domestic abuse shelters ($N = 69$, 34.5%; see Balkin et al., 2014). Participants included 165 (82.5%) females and 35 (17.5%) males, with a mean age of 33.33 years ($SD = 14.21$ years). The following ethnic breakdown was reported: white ($n = 115$, 57.5%), Latino/a ($n = 47$, 23.5%), African American ($n = 18$, 9.5%), Asian ($n = 8$, 4%), other ($n = 8$, 4%), and missing ($n = 4$, 2%).

Evidence of Test Content

The development of the FRI was theoretically aligned with the FRM (Balkin et al., 2009). The FRM illustrates a process of interpersonal or intrapersonal forgiveness based on a Jewish conceptualization of forgiveness. Despite the FRM being derived from an understanding of religious/spiritual dimensions of forgiveness specific to Judaism, the FRM may be applied to a variety of multicultural contexts (Balkin et al.,

2014). The FRM includes four sequential stages to examine viewpoints of an issue related to conflict and forgiveness and employs a decision-making model toward interpersonal or intrapersonal forgiveness. In addition, two expert reviewers with publications in the area of forgiveness reviewed the items. Minimal changes were made to revise the items to reflect clear and concise description of the FRM.

For a comprehensive review of the theoretical underpinnings of the FRM, see the following:

Balkin, R. S., Freeman, S. J., & Lyman, S. R. (2009). Forgiveness, reconciliation, and mechila: Integrating the Jewish concept of forgiveness in to clinical practice. *Counseling and Values, 53,* 153–160.

For a detailed review of the psychometric properties of the FRI, see the following:

Balkin, R. S., Harris, N., Freeman, S. J., & Huntington, S. (2014). The Forgiveness Reconciliation Inventory: An instrument to process through issues of forgiveness and conflict. *Measurement and Evaluation in Counseling and Development, 47,* 3–13. doi:10.1177/0748175613497037

Evidence Based on Response Processes

Each of the four stages of the FRM is represented by a statement followed by six opposing adjective pairs. "The items for the FRI were designed using semantic differentials (Osgood, 1957), establishing dichotomous choices of opposing adjectives that represent each stage and are aligned with the FRM" (Balkin et al., 2014, p. 6). Five checkboxes separate each of the opposing adjectives, representing scores of 5 to 1 from the leftmost box to the rightmost box. With six items in each of the four sections ranging from 5 to 1, a composite score for each section will range from 6 to 30. Higher scores are associated with more positive feelings toward the offender and suggesting an interpersonal process toward forgiveness, and lower scores are associated with more negative feelings toward the offender and suggesting an intrapersonal process to forgiveness.

Hence, there are 24 items with six items per stage. Each group of six items falls under a preliminary statement (see Appendix A).

For the collaborative exploration stage, participants are asked to identify adjectives for the following statement: "Regarding the person who harmed me, I feel. . . ." A sample adjective pair is *peaceful–hostile.* For the role of reconciliation stage, participants are asked to identify adjectives for the following statement: "Re-establishing a relationship with the person who harmed me would be. . . ." A sample adjective pair is *compassionate–unfeeling*. For the remorse/change stage, participants are asked to identify adjectives for the following statement: "The person who harmed me is. . . ." A sample adjective pair is *honest–deceitful*. For the final stage, outcome, participants are asked to identify adjectives for the following statement: "In the future, my relationship with the person who harmed me is likely to be. . . ." A sample adjective pair is *beneficial–useless* (Balkin et al., 2014, p. 6).

Evidence of Internal Structure

A confirmatory factor analysis (CFA) was conducted using 200 participants to establish factor structure given the instrument was aligned with a specific theory and items developed for a specific phase within each theory. The hypothesized model, therefore, included four first-order latent variables aligned with the specific phases of the FRM: Collaborative Exploration, Role of Reconciliation, Remorse/Change, and Choosing an Outcome. Each of the four latent variables included six indicators. The hypothesized model was statistically significant, $\chi^2(246) = 693.17$, $p < .001$. The fit indices indicated a mediocre to good fit for the data, CFI = .88, TLI = .87, SRMR = .069 (Balkin et al., 2014; Dimitrov, 2012). An alternative model was tested to see if a better fit could be obtained by accounting for correlated error variances. The alternative model did show an improvement from the hypothesized model, $\chi^2(244) = 598.49$, $p < .001$. The fit indices indicated an acceptable fit for the data, CFI = .91, TLI = .90, SRMR = .069. Unstandardized beta weights ranged from .71 to .85 for Collaborative Exploration, .62 to .84 for Role of Reconciliation, .66 to .89 for Remorse/Change, and .74 to .91 for Choosing an Outcome. Reliability estimates using Cronbach's alpha for the scores of this normative sample were as follows (Balkin et al., 2014):

- .90, Collaborative Exploration;
- .88, Role of Reconciliation;
- .92, Remorse/Change;
- .93, Choosing an Outcome;

In addition, differential item functioning was assessed to evaluate how clinical and nonclinical populations might respond differently on the FRI.

A statistically significant difference was noted between clinical and nonclinical participants, $\lambda = .885$, $F(4, 195) = 6.22$, $p < .001$. A moderate effect size was noted, accounting for 11.5% of the variance in the model. Centroid means for the discriminant functions indicated that the clinical group (.49) had significantly higher values across the four FRI subscales than the nonclinical group (–.26), suggesting that participants in the clinical group identified more negative feelings or attributes toward those who harmed them (Balkin et al., 2014, p. 8).

Evidence of Relationships to Other Variables

Correlational analyses were conducted to identify convergent and discriminant evidence in other forgiveness measures. Small to moderate correlations would identify similarities to other existing measures, while also demonstrating unique elements of the FRI. Two instruments, the *Forgiveness Scale* and the *Forgiveness Likelihood Scale* (Rye et al., 2001) were used in these analyses. As noted in Chapter 9, the *Forgiveness Scale* and the *Forgiveness Likelihood Scale* were designed as part of a study to evaluate forgiveness from college women wronged in a relationship. The normative sample of the FRI was broader, with no specific requirements beyond being older than 18 years.

Correlations with Rye's (2001) *Forgiveness Likelihood Scale* were small, ranging from −.09 to −.23, which was not unexpected given that the FRI was not designed to evaluate the likelihood of forgiveness. The negative relationship indicated that a higher likelihood to forgive an offender was associated with a higher likelihood for the victim to choose an intrapersonal process. A multiple regression analysis confirmed this hypothesis, demonstrating a statistically significant relationship between the FRI scales and the *Forgiveness Likelihood Scale* and a small to moderate effect size, $F(4, 165) = 4.54$, $p < .05$, $R^2 = .10$ (Balkin et al., 2014).

Correlations with Rye's (2001) *Forgiveness Scale* ranged from −.32 to −.67. Using canonical correlation, a statistically significant relationship was found between the FRI scales and the *Forgiveness Scale* subscales. The first canonical root was significant, $\lambda = .49$, $F(8, 326) = 17.62$, $p < .001$, accounting for 49% ($r_c = .70$) of the variance in the model. The canonical variate included scores on all four subscales of the FRI, with correlations ranging from −.63 to −.97, and on both subscales of the Forgiveness Scale, with correlations ranging from .69 to .97. From this analysis, we found that positive attributes on the FRI were correlated with higher degrees of forgiveness toward an offender (Balkin et al., 2014).

Evidence of Consequences of Testing

A scoring profile was developed to provide a visual representation of the scores on the FRI. Examples of potential profiles were addressed in Chapter 8. The user should keep in mind that the FRI is not a diagnostic instrument but rather a process instrument, used to aid and facilitate discussions or introspection related to conflict and forgiveness. The scoring profile may aid the user in identifying conflicting beliefs and emotions related to forgiveness and provide guidance to pursuing interpersonal or intrapersonal forgiveness.

Conclusion

The development of the FRI was informed by the FRM (Balkin et al., 2009) and may be used to help individuals address feelings and beliefs related to conflict and forgiveness. Validation of the FRI is in line with contemporary standards for psychological testing (see American Educational Research Association, American Psychological Association, & National Council of Measurement in Education, 2014). The FRI may be useful for clinicians as an adjunct to the counseling process or self-administered and serves as a way to explore feelings and beliefs related to interpersonal and intrapersonal forgiveness.

REFERENCES

American Counseling Association. (2014). *ACA code of ethics.* Alexandria, VA: Author.

American Educational Research Association, American Psychological Association, & National Council of Measurement in Education. (2014). *Standards for educational and psychological testing.* Washington, DC: American Educational Research Association.

Aquino, K., Tripp, T. M., & Bies, R. J. (2007). "Getting even or moving on? Power, procedural justice, and types of offense as predictors of revenge, forgiveness, reconciliation, and avoidance in organizations": Correction to Aquino, Tripp, and Bies (2006). *Journal of Applied Psychology, 92*(1), 80. doi:10.1037/0021-9010.92.1.80

Associated Press. (2015, June 19). Families of victims deliver statements at Dylann Roof bond hearing. *Boston Globe.* Retrieved from https://www.bostonglobe.com/news/nation/2015/06/19/families-victims-deliver-statements-dylann-roof-bond-hearing/Yobn85Z4BTaMFnMhy8HQIJ/story.html

Balkin, R. S., Freeman, S. J., & Lyman, S. R. (2009). Forgiveness, reconciliation, and mechila: Integrating the Jewish concept of forgiveness in to clinical practice. *Counseling and Values, 53,* 153–160. http://dx.doi.org/10.1002/j.2161-007X.2009.tb00121.x

Balkin, R. S., Harris, N., Freeman, S. J., & Huntington, S. (2014). The Forgiveness Reconciliation Inventory: An instrument to process through issues of forgiveness and conflict. *Measurement and Evaluation in Counseling and Development, 47,* 3–13. doi:10.1177/0748175613497037

Balkin, R. S., & Juhnke, G. A. (2018). *Assessment in counseling: Practice and applications.* New York: Oxford University Press.

Balkin, R. S., Perepiczka, M., Sowell, S. M., Cumi, K., & Gnilka, P. G. (2016). The Forgiveness-Reconciliation Model: An empirically supported process for humanistic counseling. *Journal of Humanistic Counseling, 55,* 55–65, doi:10.1002/johc.12024

Beck, A. T. (1972). *Depression: Causes and treatment.* Philadelphia: University of Pennsylvania Press.

Blumenthal, D. R. (1998). Repentance and forgiveness. *Cross Currents, 48,* 75–82. doi:10.1300/J154v07n02_05

Bordin, E. S. (1979). The generalizability of the psychoanalytic concept of the working alliance. *Psychotherapy: Theory, Research & Practice, 16*(3), 252–260.

Branch, W. T., Jr., Torke, A., & Brown-Haithco, R. C. (2006). The importance of spirituality in African-Americans' end-of-life experiences. *Journal of General Internal Medicine, 21,* 1203–1205.

Breuer, J., & Freud, S. (2004). *Studies on hysteria.* New York: Penguin Books.

Burns, D. D. (1980). *Feeling good: The new mood therapy.* New York: William Morrow.

Burns, D. D. (1989). *The feeling good handbook: Using the new mood therapy in everyday life.* New York: William Morrow.

Casey, K. L. (1998). Surviving abuse: Shame, anger, forgiveness. *Pastoral Psychology, 46,* 223–231.

Cohen, A. B., Malka, A., Rozin, P., & Cherfas, L. (2006). Religion and unforgivable offenses. *Journal of Personality, 74,* 85–118. doi:10.1111/j.1467-6494.2005.00370.x

Davis, D. E., Ho, M. Y., Griffin, B. J., Bell, C., Hook, J. N., Van Tongeren, D. R., . . . Westbrook, C. J. (2015). Forgiving the self and physical and mental health correlates: A meta-analytic review. *Journal of Counseling Psychology, 62,* 329–335. doi:10.1037/cou0000063

de Shazer, S. (1985). *Keys to solutions in brief therapy.* New York: W. W. Norton.

Diamond, S. A. (1996). *Anger, madness and the daimonic.* Albany: State University of New York Press.

Dimitrov, D. M. (2012). *Statistical methods for validation of assessment scale data in counseling and related fields.* Alexandria, VA: American Counseling Association.

Duffey, T., & Somody, C. (2011). The role of relational-cultural theory in mental health counseling. *Journal of Mental Health Counseling, 33*(3), 223–242. https://doi-org.umiss.idm.oclc.org/10.17744/mehc.33.3.c10410226u275647

Duncan, B. L. (2014). *On becoming a better therapist.* Washington, DC: American Psychological Association.

Eckstein, J. (2011). Reasons for staying in intimately violent relationships: Comparisons of men and women and messages communicated to self and others. *Journal of Family Violence, 26*(1), 21–30. doi:10.1007/s10896-010-9338-0

Edwards, K. M., Gidycz, C. A., & Murphy, M. J. (2011). College women's stay/leave decisions in abusive dating relationships: A prospective analysis of an expanded investment model. *Journal of Interpersonal Violence, 26*(7), 1446–1462. https://doi-org.umiss.idm.oclc.org/10.1177/0886260510369131

Ellis, A. (1996). *Better, deeper, and more enduring brief therapy: The rational emotive behavior therapy approach.* Bristol, PA: Brunner/Mazel.

Enright, R. D. (2001). *Forgiveness is a choice.* Washington, DC: American Psychological Association.

Enright, R. D., Freedman, S., & Rique, J. (1998). The psychology of interpersonal forgiveness. In R. D. Enright & J. North (Eds.), *Exploring forgiveness* (pp. 46–62). Madison: University of Wisconsin Press.

Enright, R. D., & the Human Development Study Group. (1991). The moral development of forgiveness. In W. Kurtines & J. Gewirtz (Eds.), *Handbook of moral behavior and development* (Vol. 1, pp. 123–152). Hillsdale, NJ: Erlbaum.

Enright, R. D., & Zell, R. L. (1989). Problems encountered when we forgive one another. *Journal of Psychology and Christianity, 8*(1), 52–60.

Federal Bureau of Investigations (FBI). (n.d.). *Defining a hate crime.* Retrieved on June 16, 2019, from https://www.fbi.gov/investigate/civil-rights/hate-crimes

Freud, A. (1937). *The Ego and the mechanisms of defense.* London: Hogarth Press and Institute of Psycho-Analysis.

Freud, S. (1894). *The neuro-psychoses of defence.* SE, 3: 41–61.

Freud, S. (1896). *Further remarks on the neuro-psychoses of defence.* SE, 3: 157–185.

Freud, S. (1998). *Case histories II.* London: Penguin UK.

Glasser, W. (1998). *Choice theory.* New York: HarperCollins Publishers.

Hall, J. H., & Fincham, F. D. (2005). Self-forgiveness: The step-child of forgiveness research. *Journal of Social and Clinical Psychology, 24,* 621–637.

Hamel, J. (2012). *Partner abuse state of knowledge project: Findings at a glance.* Retrieved on December 1, 2019, from http://www.domesticviolenceresearch.org/pdf/FindingsAt-a-Glance.Nov.23.pdf

Hammond, W. P., Banks, K. H., & Mattis, J. S. (2006). Masculinity ideology and forgiveness of racial discrimination among African American men: Direct and interactive relationships. *Sex Roles, 55,* 679–692. doi:10.1007/s11199-006-9123-y

Hanke, K., & Vauclair, C. M. (2016). Investigating the human value "forgiveness" across 30 countries: A cross-cultural, meta-analytical approach. *Cross-Cultural Research, 50,* 215–230. doi:10.1177/1069397116641085

Harris, N. A. (2015). *Using the forgiveness and reconciliation inventory: A qualitative inquiry examining the experiences of the process* (Order No. 3736191). Available from ProQuest Dissertations & Theses A&I. (1747126493). Retrieved from http://umiss.idm.oclc.org/login?url=https://search-proquest-com.umiss.idm.oclc.org/docview/1747126493?accountid=14588

Havighurst, R. J. (1972). *Developmental tasks and education* (3rd ed.). New York: D. McKay.

Hook, J. N., Worthington, E. L., Jr., Utsey, S. O., Davis, D. E., & Burnette, J. L. (2012). Collectivistic self-construal and forgiveness. *Counseling and Values, 57,* 109–124.

Hunter, A. (2007). Forgiveness: Hindu and Western perspectives. *Journal of Hindu-Christian Studies, 20* (Article 11). htpps://doi.org/10.7825/2164-6279.1386.

International Forgiveness Institute. (2015). *How to forgive.* Retrieved on December 23, 2018, from https://internationalforgiveness.com/need-to-forgive.htm

Jordan, J. V. (1991). The meaning of mutuality. In J. V. Jordan, A. G. Kaplan, J. B. Miller, I. P. Stiver, & J. L. Surrey (Eds.), *Women's growth in connection: Writing from the Stone Center* (pp. 81–96). New York: The Guilford Press.

Jung, C. G., & Franz, M. V. (1968). *Man and his symbols.* New York: Dell.

Khayat, R. (2013). *The education of a lifetime.* Oxford, MS: Nautilus.

Kottler, J. A. (2018). The power of storytelling to promote resilience and recovery from life's disappointments and tragedies. *Televizion.* Retrieved on August 15, 2019, from https://www.br-online.de/jugend/izi/english/publication/televizion/ 31_2018_E/Kottler-The_power_of_storytelling.pdf

Kottler, J. A., & Balkin, R. S. (2017). *Relationships in counseling and the counselor's life.* Alexandria, VA: American Counseling Association.

Kottler, J. A., & Balkin, R. S. (2020). *Myths, misconceptions, and invalid assumptions about counseling.* New York: Oxford University Press.

Kübler-Ross, E. (2005). *On grief and grieving: Finding the meaning of grief through the five stages of loss.* New York: Simon & Schuster.

Lambert, M. J. (Ed.) (2013). *Bergin and Garfield's handbook of psychotherapy and behavior change* (6th ed.). New York: Wiley.

Macaskill, A. (2005). Defining forgiveness: Christian clergy and general population perspectives. *Journal of Personality, 73,* 1237–1266. https://doi-org.umiss.idm.oclc.org/10.1111/j.1467-6494.2005.00348.x

Martin, J. W., & Cushman, F. (2016). Why we forgive what can't be controlled. *Cognition, 147,* 133–143. doi:10.1016/j.cognition.2015.11.008

McAdams, C. A., & Foster, V. A. (2000). Client suicide: Its frequency and impact on counselors. *Journal of Mental Health Counseling, 22,* 107. doi:10.1002/j.1556-6978.1999.tb01787.x

Menahem, S., & Love, M. (2013). Forgiveness in psychotherapy: The key to healing. *Journal of Clinical Psychology, 69*(8), 829–835. https://doi-org.umiss.idm.oclc.org/10.1002/jclp.22018

Mullet, E., & Azar, F. (2009). Apologies, repentance, and forgiveness: A Muslim-Christian comparison. *International Journal for the Psychology of Religion, 19*(4), 275–285. https://doi-org.umiss.idm.oclc.org/10.1080/10508610903146274

National District Attorney Association. (2019). *State criminal incest statutes.* Retrieved on January 5, 2019, from https://ndaa.org/

Norcross, J. C., & Lambert, M. J. (2011). Psychotherapy relationships that work II. *Psychotherapy, 48*(1), 4–8. http://dx.doi.org/10.1037/a0022180

Omo-Osagie, S. I., II. (2007). "Their souls made the whole": Negro spirituals and lessons in healing and atonement. *Western Journal of Black Studies, 31*(2), 34–41.

Osgood, C. E., Suci, G., & Tannenbaum, P. (1957). *The measurement of meaning*. Urbana: University of Illinois Press.

Powell, W., Banks, K. H., & Mattis, J. S. (2017). Buried hatchets, marked locations: Forgiveness, everyday racial discrimination, and African American men's depressive symptomatology. *American Journal of Orthopsychiatry, 87,* 646–662. doi:10.1037/ort0000210

Power, F. C. (1994). Commentary. *Human Development, 37,* 81–85.

Puffett, N. K. & Gavin, C. (2004, April). *Predictors of program outcome & recidivism at the Bronx Misdemeanor Domestic Violence Court, Center for Court Innovation.* Retrieved on May 12, 2019, from https://www.courtinnovation.org/sites/default/files/predictorsbronxdv.pdf

Rakovec-Felser, Z. (2014). Domestic violence and abuse in intimate relationship from public health perspective. *Health Psychology Research, 2*(3), 62–67. doi:10.4081/hpr.2014.1821

Raven, B. H. (1965). Social influence and power. In I. D. Steiner & M. Fishbein (Eds.), *Current studies in social psychology* (pp. 371–382). New York: Holt, Rinehart, Winston.

Raven, B. H., & French, J. (1959). The bases of social power. In D. Cartwright (Ed.), *Studies in social power* (pp. 150–167). Ann Arbor, MI: Institute for Social Research.

Rogers, C. R. (1961). *On becoming a person*. Houghton Mifflin.

Rye, M. S., Loiacono, D. M., Folck, C. D., Olszewski, B. T., Heim, T. A., & Madia, B. P. (2001). Evaluation of the psychometric properties of two forgiveness scales. *Current Psychology, 20,* 260–277.

Rye, M. S., Pargament, K. I., Ali, M. A., Beck, G. L., Dorff, E. N., Hallisey, C., . . . Williams, J. G. (2000). Religious perspectives on forgiveness. In M. E. McCullough, K. I. Pargament, & C. E. Thoresen (Eds.), *Forgiveness: Theory, research, and practice.* (pp. 17–40). New York: Guilford Press.

Sanoff, A. P. (1986, October 27). One must not forget. *US News and World Report*.

Schneiderman, N., Ironson, G., & Siegel, S. D. (2005). Stress and health: Psychological, behavioral, and biological determinants. *Annual Review of Clinical Psychology, 1,* 607–628. doi:10.1146/annurev.clinpsy.1.102803.144141

Scobie, E. D., & Scobie, G. E. W. (1998). Damaging events: The perceived need for forgiveness. *Journal for the Theory of Social Behaviour, 28,* 373–401. http://dx.doi.org/10.1080/13557858.2012.655264

Shedler, J. (2018). Changing the topic does not change the facts. *Lancet, 5,* 539. http://dx.doi.org/10.1016/S2215-0366(18)30093-2

Stangor, C., Jhangiani, R., & Tarry, H. (2014). *Principles of social psychology*. Minneapolis: Open Textbook Library.

Sternthal, M. J., Williams, D. R., Musick, M. A., & Buck, A. C. (2012). Religious practices, beliefs, and mental health: Variations across ethnicity. *Ethnicity & Health, 17,* 171–185.

Strelan, P., Di Fiore, C., & Prooijen, J. V. (2017). The empowering effect of pun-ishment on forgiveness. *European Journal of Social Psychology, 47*(4), 472–487. https://doi-org.umiss.idm.oclc.org/10.1002/ejsp.2254

Strelan, P., Feather, N., & McKee, I. (2011). Retributive and inclusive justice goals and forgiveness: The influence of motivational values. *Social Justice Research, 24*(2), 126–142. https://doi-org.umiss.idm.oclc.org/10.1007/s11211-011-0132-9

Tavernise, S. (2017, August 26). The two Americans. *New York Times.* Retrieved from https://www.nytimes.com/interactive/2017/08/26/us/fort-smith-arkansas-mosque-vandalism-and-forgiveness.html

Tripathi, A., & Mullet, E. (2010). Conceptualizations of forgiveness and forgivingness among Hindus. *International Journal for the Psychology of Religion, 20*(4), 255–266. https://doi-org.umiss.idm.oclc.org/10.1080/10508619.2010.507694

US Department of Justice. (2012). *National crime victimization survey, 2006–2010.* Retrieved on December 1, 2019, from https://www.bjs.gov/content/pub/pdf/vnrp0610.pdf

Valdez, C. E., Ban Hong (Phylice) Lim, & Lilly, M. M. (2013). "It's going to make the whole tower crooked": Victimization trajectories in IPV. *Journal of Family Violence, 28*(2), 131–140. https://doi-org.umiss.idm.oclc.org/10.1007/s10896-012-9476-7

VanderWeele, T. J. (2018). Is forgiveness a public health issue? *American Journal of Public Health, 108*(2), 189–190. https://doi-org.umiss.idm.oclc.org/10.2105/AJPH.2017.304210

Vanheule, S., Desmet, M., Meganck, R., Inslegers, R., Willemsen, J., De Schryver, M., & Devisch, I. (2014). Reliability in psychiatric diagnosis with the DSM: Old wine in new barrels. *Psychotherapy and Psychosomatics, 83,* 313–314. doi:10.1159/000358809

Wade, N. G., Kidwell, J. E. M., Hoyt, W. T., & Worthington, E. L., Jr. (2014). Efficacy of psychotherapeutic interventions to promote forgiveness: A meta-analysis. *Journal of Consulting & Clinical Psychology, 82*(1), 154–170. doi:10.1037/a0035268

Walker, D. F., & Gorsuch, R. L. (2002). Forgiveness within the Big Five personality model. *Personality and Individual Differences, 32,* 1127–1137. doi:10.1016/S0191-8869(00)00185-9

Walker, L. E. (1979). *The battered woman.* New York: Harper & Row.

Waller, W. (1938). *The family, a dynamic interpretation.* New York: Dryden Press.

Walton, E. (2005). Therapeutic forgiveness: Developing a model for empowering victims of sexual abuse. *Clinical Social Work Journal, 33,* 193–207.

Wenzel, M., & Okimoto, T. G. (2010). How acts of forgiveness restore a sense of justice: Addressing status/power and value concerns raised by transgressions. *European Journal of Social Psychology, 40*(3), 401–417.

Wenzel, M., & Okimoto, T. G. (2012). The varying meaning of forgive-ness: Relationship closeness moderates how forgiveness affects feelings of justice. *European Journal of Social Psychology, 42*(4), 420–431. doi:10.1002/ejsp.1850

Worthington, E. (2018). *REACH forgiveness of others.* Retrieved on December 23, 2018, from http://www.evworthington-forgiveness.com/reach-forgiveness-of-others

Worthington, E. L., Jr., & Wade, N. G. (1999). The psychology of unforgiveness and forgiveness and implications for clinical practice. *Journal of Social and Clinical Psychology, 18*(4), 385–418. doi:10.1521/jscp.1999.18.4.385

Wuthnow, R. (2000). How religious groups promote forgiving: A national study. *Journal for the Scientific Study of Religion, 39*, 125–139. http://dx.doi.org/10.1111/0021-8294.00011

INDEX

Tables and figures are indicated by *t* and *f* following the page number

For the benefit of digital users, indexed terms that span two pages (e.g., 52–53) may, on occasion, appear on only one of those pages.